3230161361

GW01558262

WITHDRAWN

Passage Planning Guidelines

3rd Edition

Witherby Seamanship International
A Division of Witherby Publishing Group Ltd

4 Dunlop Square, Livingston, Edinburgh, EH54 8SB, Scotland, UK

Tel No: +44(0)1506 463 227 - Fax No: +44(0)1506 468 999

Email: info@emailws.com - Web: www.witherbyseamanship.com

First edition published 1997
Second edition published 2014
Third edition published 2015

ISBN: 978-1-85609-565-5

British Library Cataloguing in Publication Data

A catalogue record for this book is available from the British Library.

Acknowledgement

This product has been derived in part from material obtained from the UK Hydrographic Office with the permission of the UK Hydrographic Office.

Notice

The UK Hydrographic Office (UKHO) and its licensors make no warranties or representations, express or implied, with respect to this product. The UKHO and its licensors have not verified the information within this product or quality assured it.

Printed by The Print Network, Penrith, UK

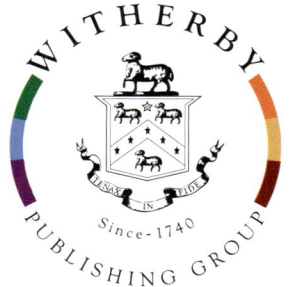

Published by

Witherby Publishing Group Ltd
4 Dunlop Square, Livingston,
Edinburgh, EH54 8SB,
Scotland, UK

Tel No: +44(0)1506 463 227
Fax No: +44(0)1506 468 999

Email: info@emailws.com
Web: www.witherbys.com

Foreword

In 1997, Captain David Salmon was tasked with the preparation of a booklet to be used as a guide for ships' navigating officers when preparing a passage plan.

Captain Salmon was a former Navigation Superintendent who had also been involved in the preparation of a paper, for the then Dept of Transport (now the UK Maritime and Coastguard Agency), on the subject of passage planning on board ship.

The primary objective of the booklet is to assist with the appraisal and planning stages of the passage planning process.

It contains a new section on ECDIS passage planning. However, it must be well understood by all that the fundamentals and principles of passage planning remain unchanged when using electronic charts, and that the navigating officer must still thoroughly research the route, recording all his workings, notes, charts, timings, etc in either a work book or an accepted electronic log.

This publication in no way attempts to define the rights or wrongs as to how the Master of any vessel conducts the sole navigation of his own vessel and only serves as a reference and information document to assist responsible persons who may require clarification on certain aspects of passage planning.

Abbreviations

ALL - Admiralty List of Lights

ALRS - Admiralty List of Radio Signals

APC - Appropriate Portfolio of Paper Charts

ATT - Admiralty Tide Tables

CATZOC - Category of Zone of Confidence in data

DW - Deep Water Route

ECA - Emission Control Area

ECDIS - Electronic Chart Data Information System

ENC - Electronic Navigational Chart

MLC - Maritime Labour Convention from the International Labour Organization (ILO)

NTM - Notice to Mariners

PSSA - Particularly Sensitive Sea Area

RCDS - Raster Chart Display System

SECA - Sulphur Emission Control Area

SMS - Safety Management System

SOG - Speed Over the Ground

STCW - Standards for Training and Certification of Watchkeepers

T&Ps - Temporary and Preliminary Notices

TSS - Traffic Separation Scheme

UKC - Under Keel Clearance

VTS - Vessel Traffic Service

XTL - Cross Track Limit

Contents

SECTION 3 – Annexes   **99**

SECTION 1

Traditional and Paper Based Passage Planning

1   The Need for a Comprehensive Passage Plan

The intended voyage shall be planned in advance, taking into consideration all pertinent information and any course laid down shall be checked before the voyage commences.

STCW A-VIII/2-3

The need for voyage and passage planning applies to all vessels.

Ships undertake different voyages depending on their size/trade. Decisions affecting the route taken are further influenced by the requirements of the ship's owner or charterer and the specific measures that may be required for ships carrying hazardous cargoes in coastal waters or where there are environmental considerations such as emission control areas.

It is customary on most deep sea ships for the Master to delegate the initial responsibility for preparing the passage plan to the navigating officer. A detailed passage plan will be submitted for the Master's assessment before the vessel's departure. Should the final destination be changed, an updated version of the plan should be prepared.

> **The necessity to prepare and follow a passage plan is well established on board vessels and is detailed in SOLAS Chapter V Regulation 34 and in IMO Resolution A.983(21). This is also a requirement of a vessel's SMS, under ISM clause 7 regarding shipboard operations. The general principles of passage planning are contained within STCW II/I (operational) and II/2 (management) levels.**

The SMS guidelines should assist the Master and OOW in the requirements for passage planning.

Safe navigation and avoidance of dangerous situations

1   Prior to proceeding to sea, the master shall ensure that the intended voyage has been planned using the appropriate nautical charts and nautical publications for the area concerned, taking into account the guidelines and recommendations developed by the Organization.

2   The voyage plan shall identify a route which:

.1   takes into account any relevant ships' routeing systems;

.2   ensures sufficient sea room for the safe passage of the ship throughout the voyage;

.3   anticipates all known navigational hazards and adverse weather conditions; and

.4   takes into account the marine environmental protection measures that apply, and avoids, as far as possible, actions and activities which could cause damage to the environment.

Part 2 Voyage planning

1.2.1   General Requirements

The intended voyage shall be planned in advance, taking into consideration all pertinent information, and any course laid down shall be checked before the voyage commences.

The chief engineer officer shall, in consultation with the master, determine in advance the needs of the intended voyage, taking into consideration the requirements for fuel, water,

1.1 SOLAS V - Regulation 34

1.2 STCW Code – Part A-VIII – Watchkeeping

lubricants, chemicals, expendable and other spare parts, tools, supplies and any other requirements.

1.2.2 Planning Prior to Each Voyage

Prior to each voyage, the master of every ship shall ensure that the intended route from the port of departure to the first port of call is planned using adequate and appropriate charts and other nautical publications necessary for the intended voyage, containing accurate, complete and up-to-date information regarding those navigational limitations and hazards which are of a permanent or predictable nature and which are relevant to the safe navigation of the ship.

1.3 Guidance on Approaching a Traditional Paper Based Passage Plan

Passage planning is not just about creating a set of lines, waypoints, courses and distances on a navigational chart, nor is it about collecting notes into text books, notepads and folders. To be effective, passage planning must be viewed as an opportunity to share relevant voyage information, and the detailed actions at its different stages, by creating a mental and physical model. Passage planning is a fundamental and safety critical skill and the safe passage of a vessel and its crew depends on it.

All navigational data should be treated with appropriate caution, especially when passage planning. The navigating officer should check the sources for validity and ensure that only information from trusted sources, that meet the expected accuracy standards, is used. All working should be cross checked and double checked to ensure consistency.

No two passages are likely to be exactly the same, even if they appear to be that way. The navigating officer responsible for passage planning should be given the time and resources for planning, as well as opportunities for discussions with the Master about complex manoeuvres. Basic guidance on procedures and documentation requirements should be as per the safety management system (SMS). All limits should be applied as per the SMS and the Master's standing orders. The starting point is the receipt of clear instructions from the Master, which is also when the exact names of the ports should be checked. The process should then involve checking up requirements from the Chief Engineer and the Chief Officer relating to draught, bunkers, MARPOL discharges from the vessel, ballast water exchange and stability/stresses at various stages of the voyage.

For a coastal passage, review of all relevant 'Sailing Directions' should be undertaken and the route should be chosen considering navigational safety. Local knowledge should be sought at the planning stage by using pilots, sailing directions and marine safety information (MSI). For routes across the ocean, a review of guidance in 'The Ocean Passages of the World' and the 'Routeing Chart' for the ocean area, considering the time of the year, should be undertaken. Any restrictions stated within the publications should be promptly brought to the Master's attention.

For any other voyage type, start by plotting the different types of routes on a gnomonic chart. Check to see if the routes pass over, or dangerously close to, any land or islands. If a great circle route is the chosen route, select waypoints at 5° intervals of longitude and transfer these to an ocean scale Mercator chart and routeing chart of the area. On the Mercator chart, check for navigational hazards and on the routeing chart check for loadline zones and elements of nature, such as: currents, winds, TRS activity, ice limits, gales, reduced visibility, etc. The appraisal process can then begin once this and other relevant information is available.

Remember, that appraisal is not just about gathering information, but is more about the effect of such information on the safety and efficiency of the voyage.

The navigating officer should now be in a position to present various route options to the Master, who will choose one or more options for detailed planning to be undertaken. This choice will depend on time of the year and the weather and currents the vessel is going to encounter. Route planning should take advantage of favourable conditions, wherever possible, and avoid adverse conditions while remembering that a longer route may be more efficient and safe. Using vessel draught, required manoeuvres and turns, speed, weather and sea state, the navigating officer should set minimum under keel clearance (UKC) requirements for all stages of the voyage. Navigators should always question the integrity of information used in passage planning and navigation, particularly with regards to UKC.

The navigating officer should identify the relevant and largest scale charts and publications relating to the intended and planned voyage and check that the vessel holds the current editions. All charts and publications should be corrected up to date to the latest NTM, along with all T&Ps and existing navigational warnings. It is also important to note the datum of all the charts and to comment on the corrections to be applied to positions. The source data should be reviewed carefully for the year, scale and method of survey, as unlike ECDIS, paper charts and documents have no ability to give any warnings relating to safety. All areas must be checked for the required safety limits.

The navigating officer should now revisit the 'Sailing Directions' and 'The Ocean Passages of the World' to look for finer details relating to the voyage. The charts should be reviewed in detail, using a magnifying glass to check up all symbols and legends clearly. Do not hesitate to refer to BA5011 for symbols and abbreviations and investigate areas where depths are likely to change but no warnings are likely to be given about those changes in a timely enough manner. Having reviewed the chart, mark all the no-go areas and hatch these out on all applicable charts based on the UKC requirements worked out earlier. Obtain as accurate an ETD as possible for pilot, tides, weather and tidal streams.

Most navigating officers may start planning as an outline route on small scale charts, but it is ideal to select the departure, landfall and other waypoints on the largest scale charts and transfer these to small scale charts for building up the outline route. Note that there are going to be many other ships in the area wanting to use the shortest route and they may be converging to the same point (especially around headlands, TSS, etc) so the routes of such vessels are going to be very similar. With that in mind, and using a risk based approach, it is better to position the route away from the usual convergence points to avoid unnecessary close quarters with other traffic. Similarly, sufficient sea room should be available in convergent areas for executing any necessary avoiding actions. Risk assessments should be completed and documented for all critical stages of the passage. Planning ahead helps identify the risks and allows the navigator a better control over the vessel and the safety of navigation; but do note that while many risks can be anticipated, many cannot. Planning should allow you to anticipate important events like making landfall, passage through narrow waters and times for making critical course changes.

Once the route has been outlined and checked for safety and efficiency, the track must be finalised on all charts. Particular attention must be given to turns from wheel over to points where the vessel joins the next course line. Alongside this task, all the tidal stream, tidal height, wheel over distances, squat, light ranges, radar detection range calculations should be performed. The charts should be marked clearly with, but not limited to, the following: true tracks along with the value of the True and Magnetic courses, margins of safety, distances on each leg, wheel over points, waypoints, distance to go at each waypoint, points suitable for parallel indexing (PI) along with cross index ranges, points suitable for position fixing, marks and values for clearing bearings, extreme distances at which lights can be sighted, extreme ranges at which radar can detect charted objects, lines of contours for echo-sounder use, contingency anchorages, contingency plans, abort points, points of no return, reporting and communications points, pilotage points, etc. The monitoring points at critical stages should be annotated clearly with 'not less than' (NLT) or 'not more than' (NMT) bearings and distances. Advance warning of the hazards appearing ahead/around should be stated on the chart.

Instructions on how to apply the plan, along with details and instructions relating to it, should be stated clearly in all passage plan paperwork and notebooks. Details of pilotage and manoeuvres should be fully covered. Methods of determining errors and obtaining warnings and forecasts should be stated clearly.

Passage plans should take into account the characteristics of the vessel, including draught, manoeuvrability, squat, mechanical risks and manning levels. Consideration should be given to the need to execute manoeuvres at flood, ebb or slack conditions. The plan should also include the speeds, UKC, effects of current/tidal streams/winds, position fixing interval and methods, requirements for additional watchkeepers, engine status, anchor readiness, for each leg of the voyage. In addition, the passage plan should be marked with information on fishing grounds, MARPOL areas, offshore activity areas, wind farm activity areas, routeing schemes, warning and precautionary areas, where anchoring is prohibited, density of traffic with flow patterns, submarine cables and pipelines and areas of special significance.

The instructions for watchkeeping officers should be added to the passage plan in different ways, depending on the location of the vessel. In cases of open ocean or coastal areas, where the vessel is well clear of the coastline and traffic is minimal, the instructions may be entered into the passage plan notebook only. The amount of detail depends upon the knowledge and experience of watchkeepers, geographic location, reliability of ship equipment/machinery, and variable conditions. Where traffic and navigational intensity starts to increase the instructions can be entered into the notebook, with a referencing system between the chart and the instructions, and the basic instructions can be briefly stated on the charts. Where the vessel enters congested waters and there will be no time to consult notebooks, etc, all relevant instructions should be entered on to the chart. Remember that the chart is for navigation and should not be over cluttered; write instructions well clear of locations where positions are to be fixed.

It is an accepted fact that a plan will be changed. A good passage plan is essential, but sometimes the plan will need to be adapted based upon new information. All contingency areas and anchorages must be appraised in full in case the vessel needs to deviate during the voyage. It should be stated clearly in the plan that, prior to approaching critical areas, the stability of the vessel should be checked and based on the actual status of tanks, with the resulting calculated draught of the vessel reported to the bridge.

2 Principles of Passage Planning

There are 4 clearly identifiable stages in any passage that a ship undertakes:

- Appraisal
- Planning

(The 1ˢᵗ two stages, ie appraisal and planning, are the stages before the ship undertakes her voyage)

- Execution
- Monitoring

(The last two stages, ie execution and monitoring, are the stages that the ship undertakes during the voyage)

Appraisal

This is the gathering of all the information available, from all relevant sources, concerning the contemplated voyage from berth to berth.

Planning

Having made the fullest possible appraisal, courses are laid off on charts, distances are calculated and a detailed passage plan is documented that covers the entire voyage from berth to berth, including areas where a pilot will be on board.

Execution

The completed passage plan being available on the bridge allows the OOW to conduct the voyage in accordance with the plan.

Monitoring

This is the monitoring and control of the vessel's progress in accordance with the plan.

2.1 Appraisal

All information that can be gathered that is relevant to the voyage should be assessed. This includes, but is not restricted to, the following:

Constituent Parts of the Voyage

The voyage may involve an ocean passage, followed by a coastal passage that necessitates passing through routeing systems such as Traffic Separation Schemes (TSS), before the final coastal pilotage leg and approach to the berth.

The Current Seagoing Condition of the Vessel

The stability of the vessel (*GM & Trim*) and draught at all stages of the voyage. The state of all relevant equipment and the seaworthiness of the vessel (*is all certification valid?*). Any operational limitations and current manoeuvring characteristics (*including turning circles and wheel over requirements*).

Characteristics of the Cargo

Any special characteristics of the cargo, particularly if hazardous.

Hours of Rest

On departure and during the contemplated voyage, will the ship be able to ensure the availability of a suitably rested crew in compliance with MLC, STCW and any hours of work requirements within the territories that the ship will visit?

Master's Standing Orders

Does the Master have any specific passage planning requirements detailed in his Standing Orders?

Company or Charterer's Requirements

Some companies (*or charterers*) may stipulate their own requirements for conducting the passage and this may involve items such as a specific distance to maintain from the grounding line at certain stages of the vessel's passage.

Weather Routeing

Will the vessel be employing the services of a weather routeing advisory service?

Charted Depth Along the Route

Ensure that there is an adequate under keel clearance (UKC) at all stages of the passage, making allowances for the effects of squat at the predicted passage speed and allowances for the height of tide where required over the charted depth.

Charts

Identify the appropriate charts for the voyage and ensure that they are of the appropriate scale, accurate and corrected up to date against the latest notices to mariners (NTM), and that any relevant temporary and preliminary (T&P) notices or radio navigational warnings have been applied.

If the largest scale charts for the voyage (*or part of the voyage*) are not on board, they must be requisitioned.

Navigational Publications

Ensure up-to-date sailing directions (*Coastal Pilots*), lists of lights (ALL) and lists of radio aids to navigation are available.

Other Publications and Sources of Information

Ensure you have access to further sources of information appropriate to the voyage. This should include, but not be limited to:

- Mariners' routeing guides
- passage planning charts
- passage planning guides
- current and tidal atlases and tide tables
- climatological, hydrographical and oceanographic data as well as other appropriate meteorological information
- available port information
- details of previous passage plans
- experience from colleagues on board.

Ships Routeing

Applicable ships' routeing and reporting systems, including vessel traffic services (VTS).

Environmental

Environmental considerations that must be taken in to account during the appraisal stage, such as whether the vessel will be sailing in special areas or emission control areas (ECAs), or any specific MARPOL requirements concerning any cargo operations planned en-route.

Traffic

Anticipated volumes of traffic that are likely to be encountered during the voyage.

Pilot

Notification and contact arrangements.

Vessel Specific

Any additional items that are specific to the type of vessel or her cargo or the sea areas that the vessel will pass through.

During appraisal, the navigating officer uses information from every possible source to plan the passage. If a vital piece of information is overlooked at this stage, it can lead to problems in the later stages of the passage plan. Because of this, a checklist (*such as the one provided in Annex A*) should be used to avoid overlooking any items of information that may later prove to be critical.

Once this information has been gathered an overall appraisal of the intended voyage can be made, which will identify all areas of danger in the vicinity of those areas where it will be possible to navigate safely.

2.2 Planning

Having appraised all the available information concerning the intended voyage, the navigating officer can (under the Master's instructions) prepare a detailed plan. This may be ocean or coastal and will include all stages of pilotage, from berth to berth.

Considerations Before Plotting Courses

- Ocean routes (*Great Circle, composite Great Circle or rhumb line*)
- meteorological (*hurricanes, typhoons, fog banks, ice or icebergs*)
- night versus day transit of key areas
- physical (*ship manoeuvring characteristics, draught*)
- environmental (*tanker routeing measures or ECAs*)
- political (*war zone areas or pirate areas*)
- economic (*owners/charterers instructions*)
- operational (*state of machinery/equipment*).

Voyage Overview

- Establish route. Draw courses on smaller scale chart(s) and discuss with the Master
- Calculate distances. These are required by the Master to calculate ETAs, bunker fuel, water, lubricants, spares and other supplies.

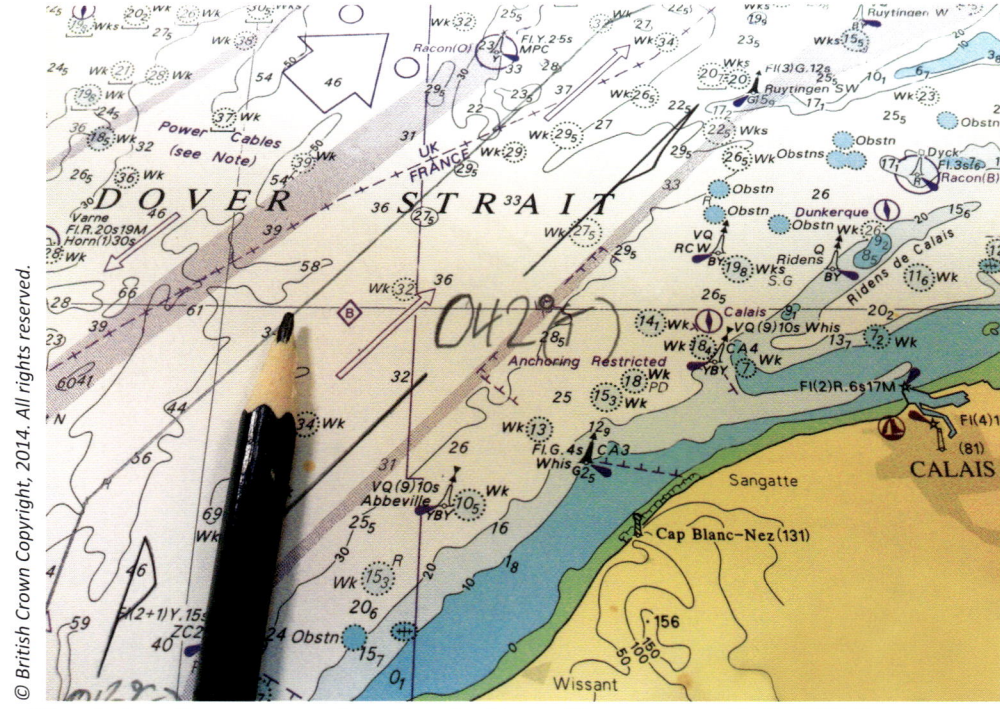

When laying off courses, consider where best to position your vessel in the TSS. For example, in the Dover Strait there is a likelihood of meeting ferries crossing from Calais to Dover, so keeping to the left hand side of the traffic lane allows plenty of room should you have to alter to starboard for crossing traffic.

While an ocean passage may involve minimal preparation in terms of courses, distances and waypoints, the navigation of coastal and pilotage waters requires concentrated preparation.

In particular, it should also define the areas where the ship must not go and the precautions required to achieve those conditions.

Charted Tracks

Plot the intended courses on the most appropriate scale charts, indicating the true course direction in 360° notation. Courses should be plotted with consideration of:

- The vessel's speed at each stage of the voyage
- proximity of navigational hazards (*Identify predicted areas of danger and mark on charts – 'no go' areas lightly pencilled and hatched*)
- manoeuvring characteristics of the vessel
- required under keel clearance (UKC)
- tidal restrictions and any requirements for timed arrival (*tidal window*)
- speed restrictions, including any areas where allowance for the increase in draught due to the effects of squat or heel when turning, need to be accounted for

- clear identification of alterations of course and, where applicable, the wheel over position taking into account the vessel's turning circle at the planned speed
- abort positions on the final approach to any constrained areas
- contingency anchorages in constrained areas.

Highlighted Items

Hazards, and any other relevant additional information, should be marked on the chart while avoiding information overload.

The following items, which will be of benefit to the bridge team, should be marked clearly:

- All areas of danger
- conspicuous points for parallel indexing
- reporting systems, including vessel traffic services (VTS)
- areas where marine environmental protection considerations apply
- positions where a change in machinery status is required
- areas where accuracy of position fixing is critical
- tidal diamonds, which can be highlighted with timely annotations made of high water (HW) at appropriate standard/secondary ports
- any VHF channels to monitor or reporting points during the transit of coastal waters and port approaches.

Items to Document in the Accompanying Passage Plan Sheet

- Method and frequency of position fixing, including primary and secondary methods and areas where maximum position fixing accuracy is required
- contingency plans to place the vessel in deeper water or identify the nearest safe anchorage that can be utilised in the event of any emergency arising
- checklists, as appropriate
- the different manning levels for watchkeeping for both the bridge and engine room are often included for the different degrees of navigational status, usually including coastal, pilotage and/or TSS passage.

An example of the information for a passage leg of a well prepared passage plan sheet is shown in Annex E - Example of Passage Planning Notes.

Plans must also account for the approach to pilot boarding grounds, where the vessel may need to adjust her course and speed to ensure that the best possible lee course is achieved.

Planning Particular to an Ocean Passage

The publication 'Ocean Passages of the World (NP 136)' provides a useful resource containing information related to ocean currents, routes, distances and meteorological information.

Routeing charts provide further navigational information, including ice limits, load line zones, prevailing wind, currents and distances between principal ports.

Voyage calculations and courses will depend on the distances, geographical region, load line restrictions and charter party requirements, but are likely to include:

- Great Circle and composite Great Circles (limiting latitude), utilising gnomic charts
- rhumb line (Mercator) sailings
- loadline restrictions
- ocean currents
- anticipated/prevailing weather conditions (seasonal or otherwise).

Participation may be required in ship routeing systems, including the USCG Automated Mutual-Assistance Vessel Rescue System (AMVER).

Climatic/Meteorological

When considering an ocean crossing, consideration must be given to climatic and meteorological conditions, possibly including weather routeing services.

The following will all contribute to the decision about the route:

- Weather warnings
- anticipated and forecasted tropical revolving storms (TRS)
- prevalence of fog banks
- ice limits and type of ice, dependent on ship classification
- monsoons, depending on the time of year and area
- adverse/favourable currents.

Economics

There may be economic considerations involved in the voyage, and contained in the owner's/charterer's instructions, which may require amendments to the route, eg:

- Bunker and potable water considerations
- speed and arrival considerations (eg, virtual arrival)
- stores replenishment
- crew or riding crew transfers.

Political

Courses and plans may need to be amended to account for:

- War zones
- areas of known piracy, including East and West Africa, and the South China Sea
- naval exercises.

Environmental

Environmental considerations may involve the need to amend courses to ensure ballast water or MARPOL compliance, eg:

- Garbage discharge

- discharge of oil or oily water residues
- ballast water exchange
- local and special area requirements
- SECA compliance.

The status of equipment and machinery for the ocean passage must be established and any deficiencies factored into the route, including an updated risk assessment for the passage.

Passenger ships operating in remote areas should also refer to: IMO Resolution A.999 (25), *'Guidelines on Voyage Planning for Passenger Ships Operating in Remote Areas'*.

Planning particular to congested waterways/traffic separation schemes (TSS)

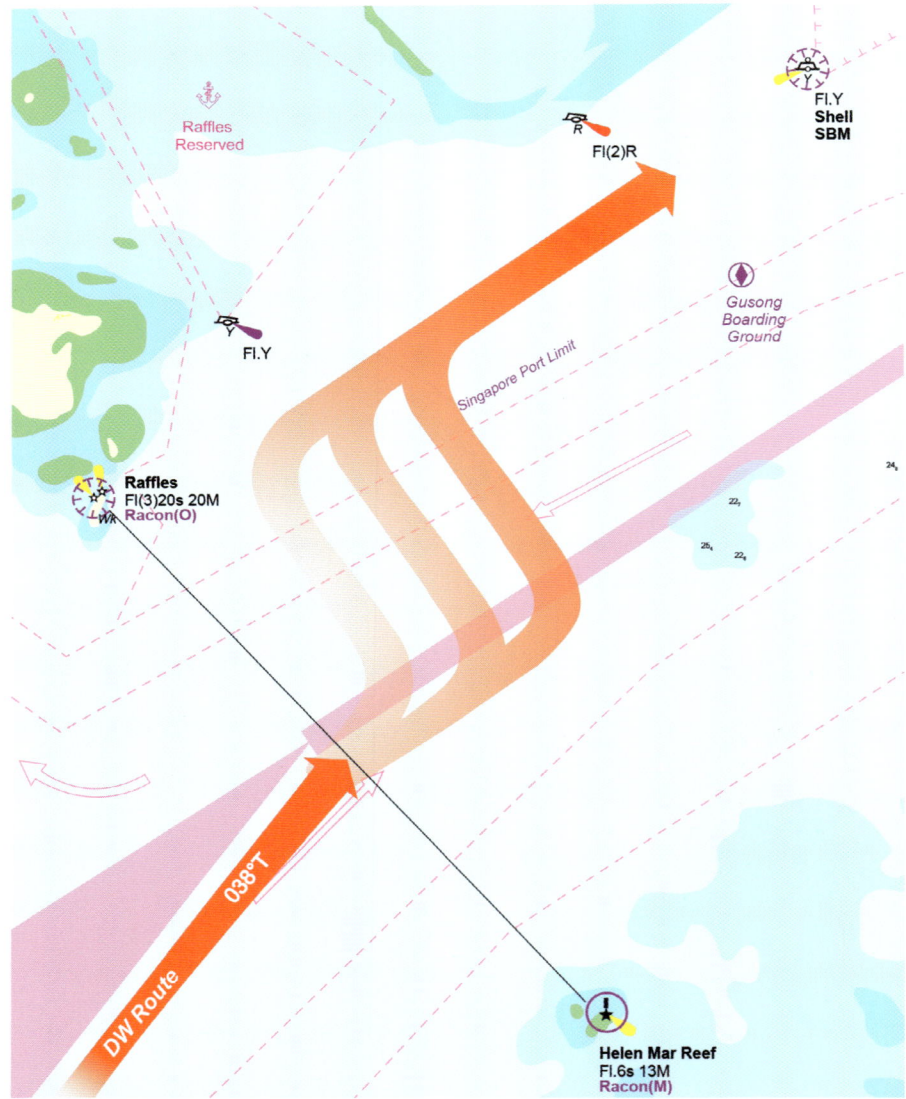

Where you have to cross a TSS, do so at right angles to the direction of traffic. However, it is best to give yourself as large a window as possible where you can safely alter to cross the TSS, such as is shown in the above chartlet where VLCCs cross the TSS south of Singapore, bound for the tanker mooring buoy.

TSSs adopted by the IMO are set out in the latest edition of the IMO publication 'Ships' Routeing'.

Of particular note when planning passages where a vessel may have to cross a TSS, is that the vessel must do so on a heading, that is as nearly as is practicable, at right angles to the direction of traffic flow. This minimises the time a crossing vessel is in the lane irrespective of the tidal stream, and should lead to a clear encounter situation with vessels passing through the main traffic lanes. Rule 10 of the Colregs applies to the conduct of all vessels in and near TSSs that have been adopted by IMO.

The British Admiralty 5000 series of charts are particularly significant to passages through congested waterways where TSSs exist. These include:

- BA 5500 English Channel and Southern North Sea
- BA 5501 Gulf of Suez
- BA 5502 Malacca and Singapore Straits
- BA 5503 Baltic Sea.

Further information can also be found in the following Witherby Seamanship publications:

- Passage Planning Guide – English Channel and Dover Straits
- Passage Planning Guide – Malacca and Singapore Straits.

Planning Particular to a Canal Transit

Transit through a canal is part of a passage plan rather than a separate passage.

A canal transit plan should be developed that contains all the relevant route information, requirements, logistics and alternative courses of action, according to defined principles and methodology.

Risk Assessment

It is vital at the passage planning stage that consideration is given to potential problems including the possibility of equipment failure. This is known as contingency planning and can be aided by proper risk assessment.

Risk assessment should follow a predetermined format in line with the ships safety management system (SMS) appropriate to each stage of the voyage. It should identify the likely hazards, the potential harm of each, evaluate the risks and specify the control measures required to manage those risks.

Completion of the Planning Stage

Once the route is complete it must be scanned/reviewed/verified to ensure that no navigational dangers have been overlooked. It will take time to complete this both on paper and on electronic charts.

Each voyage or passage plan, as well as the details of the plan, should be approved by the ships' Master prior to the commencement of the voyage or passage.

3   Conduct of the Passage (Executing and Monitoring)

Five actions set the basis for passage plan execution:

● Internal communications

● external communications

● use of physical resources

● use of human resources

● application of navigational processes.

Prior to execution, all watchkeepers will have been briefed on the passage plan and all the key requirements and manoeuvres, especially those for critical stages. The plan will have been reviewed in detail and approved by the Master. The Master should also draw the attention of the watchkeepers to the standing orders, where sections of the orders relate directly to requirements for execution and monitoring.

At the earliest stage, the departure times need to be determined as accurately as possible to help translate steaming distances into ETA at critical stages of the voyage. Prior to departure, the passage plan requires a final update with departure times and ETAs at various stages. This will allow updating of height of tide, tidal stream and wind/weather information. Furthermore, the tidal gate/window will also be decided upon to adjust departure time and ETA at critical stages. This will also allow limits to be imposed based on time of the day, visibility and flood/ebb/slack conditions for manoeuvres and/or transit.

The resources required, as per the plan, should be in place at the relevant times. These include:

- Positive reports about ship and cargo securing
- search and security checks (stowaways, unauthorised persons, contrabands, explosives, etc) of the vessel completed
- port clearance received
- bunkers and stores received
- all passengers/crew on board
- controls and main engine tests completed satisfactorily
- bridge equipment in operation
- bridge paperwork completed
- booking and embarking the pilot
- correct signals displayed
- tugs fast and mooring crew/boats standing by
- ship crew on stations
- gangway crew on station
- engine on standby.

Relevant checklists for all basic actions will need to be completed.

The plans prepared earlier by the navigating officer, for setting up the Radars and GPS/LORAN to requirements with details of passage plan and monitoring arrangements, should be set up. The required alarms such as cross track, waypoint arrival, course to steer, alter course, etc., should be set and if devices do not allow multiple settings for different legs, this exercise may have to be repeated at various stages of the voyage if different limits are to be applied. Minimum depth/UKC alarm should also be set on the echo sounder. AIS status should be changed immediately on departure.

The pilot, the Master and the bridge team must have a clear understanding of how the vessel's navigation in pilotage waters will be executed. When the pilot boards the vessel, the Master will start the information exchange. In return, the pilot will brief the Master/bridge team as to the plan they intend to follow. If there is any difference, and the Master and bridge team are in agreement as to the difference, the vessel's passage will be revised in line with the pilot's plan. The Master should review and approve the revised plan. The pilot will also brief the bridge team about the expected traffic, especially large or hampered vessels and at critical points, the tide and stream expected and how the pilot intends to use these, communication or reporting requirements, safety critical depths or points of significance, any special signals to be displayed or any byelaws or port regulations implemented recently, details of the manoeuvre for un-berthing/berthing, along with use of tugs, mooring boats, requirement for anchor team to stand by, changes required to status of machinery controls, etc.

When the pilot is on board, all helm, course and engine commands are acknowledged and executed and another officer will double check and confirm execution. For a helm order, the helmsman will repeat the pilot's advice (to confirm it was understood), apply helm and watch the indicator, when rudder angle is as per the pilot's advice the helmsman will confirm the helm position. Simultaneously, another officer will double check and confirm execution.

The vessel will be monitored using leading lights, clearing bearings, parallel indexing, passing buoys on the correct side, and plotting positions. Marking times on chart when buoys are abeam is not acceptable in lieu of positions. Any discrepancies should immediately be brought to the attention of the pilot and the Master and clarification should be sought from the pilot. All necessary actions to ensure the safety of the vessel should be taken.

The reduction of speed, necessary when embarking or disembarking a pilot, makes the vessel more vulnerable due to slow speed and change of heading, resulting in unusual sets and a possible heading towards danger. The bridge team must be extra cautious with navigation at these times. Parallel index lines should be set as minimum and maximum distances from monitoring points to keep the vessel in safe waters.

On the general route, execution and monitoring will vary with the sea area. In the open ocean the vessel should follow the great circle, composite, rhumb line route or as advised by the weather routeing service (if being used). Attempts should be made to keep to the axis of flow of ocean currents and avoid adverse currents. GPS should be used to good effect to determine track and speed made good. Care should be taken to avoid excessive set off the planned route. Celestial observations should be made to cross check the GPS positions. In addition to monitoring on the GPS, positions should also be plotted on the chart at least once a watch and an hourly log should be maintained. Observations should be continued on the ocean passage and any changes to hydrographic details should be reported. Weather reports should be received regularly and observations should be made to get an early warning of approaching adverse weather or sea state. Avoiding actions, as per contingency plans, should be executed at an early stage.

When making intermediate or final landfall, the watchkeepers should take the necessary actions to ensure compliance with the passage plan. The actions should include, but not be limited to:

- Carrying out a navigational risk assessment

- testing all controls and main engine astern

- confirm draught and stability

- using largest scale and corrected charts

- receiving and plotting navigational warnings on the chart

- receiving and updating weather information and updating its effects in the passage plan and safe navigation

- checking and verifying the gyro/compass error

- checking and verifying the general accuracy of GPS or other systems using celestial observations

- determining the current or tidal stream flow and its effect on safe navigation

- informing the engine room of any change of status or standby requirements, as well as power for deck systems

- clearing away and having anchors ready, along with crew

- having the required navigational equipment operational, along with correct set up for monitoring

- establishing bridge manning as per plan/ standing orders/SMS

- reporting to relevant authorities

- listening watch on calling frequencies etc.

For monitoring purposes when making a landfall, radars should be operated on peak performance and on long range and long pulse. Calculating the extreme range of radar detection in the passage plan may make the selected charted objects easier to locate. Parallel indexing should be commenced at an early stage. Simultaneously, visual sightings day/night should be made. When initially plotting positions using radar and visual, double check against electronic systems and check the echo sounder for matching depths and warnings of approaching shallows. Once there is confidence that the correct objects are in use for terrestrial positioning, fixing using electronic systems should become secondary. Once the position of the vessel is established with certainty, fixing should continue as per the directions and intervals specified in the passage plan. Regular comparisons should be made with DR and EP. The course made good should be verified against the course being steered to have a clear idea of the set and drift being experienced due to wind, current, tidal stream, eddies, etc. At landfall locations, traffic density will increase so it should be ensured that one of the radars is operating in sea stabilised mode, the other being in ground stabilisation. In addition to navigation, a lot of attention will be required for traffic and potential collision avoidance.

A similar approach should be adopted on the coastal passages. The objects to be used for visual and radar position fixing should be charted, as the bearings or ranges will have to be plotted on the chart from their symbols. Selected objects should be easily identifiable. Objects should be well spread to provide a good angle of cut between the position lines or ranges. The preferred angle is 90° between two objects and three marks at 60°. The angle of cut should not be less than 30°. Objects should be observable from the same compass repeater to save time between observations. Objects in transit are a good option as the bearing is not subject to compass error. The objects should be ahead of the ship rather than astern.

The watchkeepers should check the chart to identify the best objects to be used for fixing the position. Note should be made of the names of these objects and the expected bearing or range based on the projected EP or DR. At least three objects should be selected and these should be detected visually (or on radar) and identified correctly. At the required time, bearings (or ranges on radar) should be taken along with note of the exact time. Bearings of objects forward and aft of the beam should be observed first and the bearings of objects near the beam should be observed last at the required time of position. This is because the bearings abeam are likely to change more rapidly. Ranges of points abeam should be taken first as these would change the least, followed by those ahead and aft. Bearings and ranges should then be plotted on the chart and the correct symbols applied to mark the point of intersection. The time to the fix should be stated next to the symbol. Any cross-track tendency and speed/course made good should be checked. Any required course correction should be allowed. The EP/DR should be run-up for the next time of observation as set by the planned fix frequency. It is important to note that the course corrections should be well thought out and not knee-jerk reactions. Observations based on charted positions/ground track, backed by tidal stream predictions, should allow the watchkeeper to make the necessary judgements about the course to steer.

During the course of coastal passages, vessels are likely to navigate through routeing schemes. In addition to navigational constraints and the proximity of other traffic, the conduct of navigation within such schemes has to be as per Rule 10 of the IRPCS 1972. Non-compliance with the regulations can attract a penalty of up to £50,000 on summary conviction. Navigation should be well controlled and vessels should steer courses as per Rule 10 and apply effective monitoring techniques to ensure the vessel remains within the correct lane. Parallel indexing, set up in line with the lanes, would be an effective way of ensuring compliance.

It is possible that at some stage a navigator will experience a discrepancy in plotted positions. If the vessel happens to be in proximity of a hazard or a danger to navigation, the worst case position should be assumed to be correct and corrective action should be applied after a quick and careful navigational risk assessment. Such action must not cause the vessel to stand in to danger. A review should be carried out later to identify reasons for the discrepancy and the effectiveness of the corrective action taken. If there is any doubt, or insufficient time to assess the situation correctly, the watchkeeper should not hesitate to slow down the vessel or stop it completely.

All deviations from the planned route should be fully documented and charted before execution. The deviations could be weather related, based on navigational warnings, because of a discrepancy in positions or for other operational reasons. Taking short cuts is a serious matter, especially one that has not been charted or analysed for safety. It becomes an even more serious problem if effective position fixing or continuous monitoring has not taken place.

When making course changes, particularly large alterations, the vessel will be navigating inwards of the waypoint. Such turns are usually well planned and are based on the turning circle diagram/constant radius turn for a given speed and helm angle. The watchkeeper executing such a turn should follow the requirements of the plan in terms of the necessary parameters. It is also important to position the vessel correctly before commencement of the turn. If the vessel happens to be off the track, adjustments should be made to the helm angle.

There may be circumstances where either the vessel is off track or the planned route cannot be followed. There could also be circumstances arising from the standing orders, notes in passage plan or as marked on chart. If there is any doubt or problem, the Master should be immediately called to the bridge.

Throughout the voyage, the vessel should maintain proper records about the execution and monitoring. In addition to basic checklists, log book entries and VDR records, opportunities should be taken to collect pictorial or video data to support any learning from the experiences.

Finally, once the voyage is completed, the navigating officer and the Master need to review the completed voyage, especially from execution and monitoring point of view. This review should be seen as a further opportunity to determine best and marginal practice.

OOW – Items to Check During Each Navigational Watch

During each navigational watch, the OOW must pay attention to the following items:

- Availability, reliability and status of the navigational equipment on board
- primary position fixing methods
- secondary position fixing methods (including parallel indexing, echo sounder and navigational instruments)
- ETAs at the next waypoint (alteration of course and plot wheel over position where appropriate)
- marked out estimated positions on the chart based on the predicted speed over the ground (SOG) for the watch ahead of you
- margins of safety left/right of track
- anticipated tide and tidal stream effects/rates
- state of weather and the latest forecast
- the risk of restricted visibility due to sudden squalls, fog or mist
- anticipated volume of traffic
- availability of additional lookouts, such as may be needed for hand steering during periods of increased traffic volumes or restricted visibility
- availability of navigational marks with reference to a daytime versus night-time transit of critical areas
- contingency arrangements applicable
- all required reporting information at reporting points
- ETA at destination.

4   Authority to Deviate from the Plan

The owner, the charterer, the company operating the ship as defined in regulation IX/1, or any other person shall not prevent or restrict the Master of the ship from taking or executing any decision which, in the Master's professional judgement, is necessary for safety of life at sea and protection of the marine environment.

SOLAS Regulation 34-1 - Master's discretion

It is unlikely that every detail of a passage will have been anticipated, particularly in pilotage waters. This in no way detracts from the real value of the plan, which is to mark out in advance where the ship must not go and the precautions required in achieving that end. However, the OOW should not blindly follow the courses laid down on either the charts or ECDIS equipment. The OOW must be prepared to deviate from the passage plan when required in order to comply with the Colregs.

5   Navigation with a Pilot on Board

Many companies' safety management systems require testing of emergency systems and engines at the end of a sea passage, before picking up an inward pilot.

Despite the duties and obligations of pilots, their presence on board does not relieve the master or the officer in charge of the navigational watch from their duties and obligations for the safety of the ship. The master and the pilot shall exchange information regarding navigation procedures, local conditions and the ship's characteristics. The master and/or the officer in charge of the navigational watch shall co-operate closely with the pilot and maintain an accurate check on the ship's position and movement.

If in any doubt as to the pilot's actions or intentions, the officer in charge of the navigational watch shall seek clarification from the pilot and, if doubt still exists, shall notify the master immediately and take whatever action is necessary before the master arrives.'

STCW A-VIII/2-49

A pilot's up-to-date knowledge of the confined waters and port approaches where they operate requires no emphasis. However, vessels still run aground. It should be stressed that the responsibilities of the ship's navigational team do not transfer to the pilot and that the duties of the OOW remain with the officer at all times.

6   Learning from Incidents

Nawabshah

In August 1984, the 'Nawabshah' approached the western entrance to the Malacca Strait from the Bay of Bengal while on passage to the Far East. Landfall was before noon, local time, with fine weather but frequent heavy showers. During the approach the 3/O had been plotting positions using the satellite system only and, very late into the approach, effort was made to fix the ship using radar and visual means. By now the vessel had set reasonably north. The Master was summoned to the bridge at the very last moment. In a final attempt to turn a late avoiding action was of no use and the ship hit the rocks south of Rondo Island, flooding the engine room and 2 cargo compartments. While the ship sank rapidly, fortunately there was no loss of life.

In this case the passage plan was no more than a set of lines and waypoints, with no clear guidance as to which charted objects should be used at which stage for fixing or how to employ PI. There was also no guidance from the Master, either as a set of instructions on the chart or as bridge orders. It would have been useful for the plan to include clear guidance, with distances, at which radar detection, echo sounder use and visual bearings should have commenced, along with PI and the need to cross check using various means. It would also have been useful to draw attention of the watchkeepers to the possible set and effect of the wind and the necessary actions required when in doubt.

Rena

The 'Rena' ran aground on the Astrolable Reef while approaching Tauranga, in New Zealand, in 2011. The watch officers were instructed by the Master to deviate from the plan to gain advantage of current and to cut distance to reach Tauranga pilot station in time. Based on the report, it is safe to say that the navigational practices on board the 'Rena' were short of expectations. The deviations from the plan were not charted and position fixing was irregular and using GPS only. There was limited application of PI and, in the final stages before grounding, the Master took the PIs off to declutter the radar.

It is very important to chart all intended deviations after careful appraisal and risk assessment, before executing them. Assumptions should never be made that the vessel will remain safe as a result of a deviation. The watchkeepers should use a variety of methods to determine and check positions and use the echo sounder to good effect. Similarly, continuous monitoring techniques like PI should be employed to monitor the safety of the vessel. At critical stages the work of watchkeepers should be cross checked. All of this should be clearly documented in the passage plan.

COSCO Busan

The container vessel 'COSCO Busan' was navigating from the berth to the sea, with a pilot on board, in restricted visibility. At 08:30, local time, the vessel collided with one of the base towers supporting the San Francisco-Oakland Bay Bridge. It has been reported that the Master/pilot exchange before leaving the dock was not carried out properly and that there was no effective communication between the pilot and rest of the bridge team. It has also been reported that the condition and the actions of the pilot were not monitored effectively and that the Master was not assertive enough when it came to challenging the pilot. There was no effective monitoring of the ship's position or progress.

It is very important that the bridge team ensures that the passage plan (as agreed with the pilot) is being executed and that the monitoring techniques in the plan are in use. Similarly, all manoeuvres and alterations should be as per the plan. The general principles of bridge team management (BTM) should be applied at all times.

Ben-My-Chree

A RoRo passenger ferry, after leaving Heysham, grounded on a shallow patch of sand in the navigational channel. The grounding occurred nearly 1 hour before low water of the spring tides. Though the charts were up to date, changes to the seabed because of silting were not discovered or promulgated regularly by the relevant authorities.

When navigating in waters where depths are uncertain, it is better to undertake the transit at reasonable higher levels of tide so that any discrepancies in depths can be compensated for. An adjustment of the transit time in terms of execution would certainly have avoided this grounding.

COSCO Hong Kong

On passage from Xiamen to Nansha, steaming at 21 knots, the 'COSCO Hong Kong' encountered a large number of fishing vessels. The OOW's workload increased significantly and the ship was manoeuvred south of the track using the autopilot. The ship started heading for a well marked reef, which had even been highlighted as a danger in the passage plan. Because of workload, this marking was completely ignored by the OOW and the vessel ran aground over it.

It is important that the passage plan not only highlights the dangers, but that there are instructions relating to approach limits/margins of safety, manning levels and the actions required when the OOW is under stress due to conditions or traffic. The need to call the Master when the OOW is finding it difficult to keep control over the vessel or keep it safe should also be emphasised through passage plan instructions, the Master's Standing Orders and the Company's SMS.

Navigator Scorpio

This LPG carrier ran aground on the Haisborough Sand in January 2014. The investigation found a number of reasons for the grounding, including: OOW being distracted and losing situational awareness, incomplete passage plan, effects of wind and tidal stream not being taken into account, lack of application of proper navigational techniques given the vessel's proximity to danger and weakness in navigational capability of the crew.

It is imperative to apply basic principles of passage planning, navigational techniques, which should also be included and stated in the passage plan, and the BTM principles.

Unnamed Panamax Sized Vessel

A panamax vessel was transiting from one Chinese port to another. There was a military exercise taking place between the two ports. The deviation to seawards of the exercise area would have increased the distance significantly so the Master decided to deviate inwards towards the shore. Unknown to the Master, there were a number of fish farms on the deviation and, although the ship's charts were believed to be corrected and up to date, there was no indication of fish farms on the charts. The agent was asked, but no reply was received. During the deviated transit a number of fish farms were damaged.

It is important to carry out a risk assessment every time a deviation is undertaken. Where there is any uncertainty, information should be obtained from all possible (but reliable sources), including the agent. If it is not possible to receive actual charts, scans or pictures of the chart would be useful at least to identify items not otherwise on the BA or other international charts.

An Unnamed Product Tanker

A product tanker, equipped with all required navigational aids and on a regular run to a routine port, ran aground while fully loaded with a draught of 12 metres. There was a detailed passage plan available and positions were being fixed every 10 minutes using radar, visual and other means. The Master had amended the passage plan to marginally reduce the steaming distance from 6 to less than 2 nautical miles from a significant fixing point. The watch was handed over to an inexperienced OOW in a correct manner. The inexperienced OOW had to carry out quite a few arrival procedures, including calling the pilot and communicating with engine and deck teams, in addition to normal navigation. At a course alteration point, hand steering was used to alter course rather than the autopilot, but the ship's actual location was not correctly monitored. A short while later, after the Master took the con, the vessel ran aground.

The passage plan should state the manning levels required at all stages. Any amendments to the passage plan should be charted for effective monitoring. Risk assessment should be undertaken to assess changes to margins for safety or error. PI techniques should be employed and the effect of wind should be allowed for when altering courses. The OOW must follow the passage plan and the Master should comply with own standing orders as well.

Emsland

While leaving the port of Montrose, 'Emsland' ran aground during the night in adverse weather conditions. The grounding occurred shortly after disembarking the pilot, when the vessel had been set out of the channel due to wind and swell.

The passage plan must include risk assessment of the conditions to be encountered where such are not standard, especially with regards to the speed required to overcome any adverse effects of weather.

Royal Oasis

The bulk carrier 'Royal Oasis' weighed anchor off Port Talbot in August 2010. The vessel commenced a substantial turn to port as part of manoeuvre to reach the pilot station. A strong tidal stream of 3 knots was present, causing 'Royal Oasis' to hit another anchored bulk carrier the 'Berge Atlantic'.

The passage plan should include the details of tidal streams, the manoeuvres to be executed in differing conditions and how these will be influenced by wind and/or tidal stream.

Patricia

An 80 m long vessel was on passage in an area where sandbanks were common. The vessel began passage well north of the intended passage plan to compensate for a strong southerly tidal stream. The vessel was in autopilot at a speed of 9 knots while navigating over the charted depths of 8 to 9 m. At this stage the echo sounder was showing a depth of 10 m. Once the echo sounder started to show depths of 20 m or more the Master increased the speed, assuming the vessel was in clear water. A few minutes later the vessel ran aground.

It is important to detail the speeds required on all legs of the passage, state the effects of wind or tidal stream and the minimum UKC requirements. The chart should have been annotated with warnings about likely hazards and the necessary safeguards.

Blackfriars

A small product tanker was on a ballast passage from Loch Inver to Pembroke. Due to inclement weather, the Master chose to pass through Kyleakin Sound to avoid the area to the west of Isle of Skye. During this deviation the vessel grounded on the Eileanan Dubha Island.

Investigations revealed that there were numerous safety issues with BRM, passage planning and navigational techniques. All deviations should be charted with a revision of guidance to watchkeepers through the passage plan, in line with the risk assessment.

Vanguard

A seagoing tug was taking a familiar passage on the north-coast of a Scottish island to rendezvous with a vessel. During the passage, where time was not an issue, the skipper unnecessarily deviated to an inshore route between the island and some rocks and shoal patches. The skipper was unaware of the precise position of the vessel and it grounded on a submerged rock. The engine room flooded, the vessel was put on a gently sloping area, the crew evacuated and the vessel listed heavily and was declared a constructive total loss.

Any deviation should have been made after a risk assessment and should have been fully charted/documented as a passage plan. The manning levels, especially a proper lookout, should have been stated in the plan, along with monitoring techniques to be employed.

Sea Fox

This general cargo vessel was carrying packaged timber cargo on deck. The vessel's planned course had taken her downwind of shallow water. During heavy weather, the vessel encountered an exceptional wave from her starboard beam. The lashings parted and resulted in the loss and shifting of some of the deck cargo, with the vessel taking a list of 30°. Later, more cargo had to be jettisoned to improve the situation and to be able to proceed to a safe haven, where the vessel was able to re-secure the remaining cargo.

It is important to employ some of the principles of weather routeing even during coastal transits, clearly warning all watchkeepers of the effect of wind and sea state on a vessel's safety.

Jongleur

This vessel's mast struck the Gota Alvbron Bridge at Gothenburg.

The passage plan should include calculations for all relevant parameters and should clearly state the times when transits should be made for safe UKC and air clearance.

Unidentified Tanker

A chief mate on a tanker arrived on the bridge to report to the Master about securing the vessel for sea. He noticed from the chart that the vessel was taking the same outward channel as was used to arrive in to the port, which had a depth of 10.7 m. The navigating officer had negligently reversed the courses on the inbound plan. The vessel's current draught after loading was 12 m and a timely change of course saved the vessel from definite grounding.

All work on passage plans should be double checked by another person.

SECTION ②
ECDIS Passage Planning

1   Introduction

Recent decades have seen huge advances in automation within the maritime industry. This is particularly evident on vessel bridges, where banks of computer screens have largely replaced traditional navigational equipment, as computer power is harnessed to provide time saving applications. Navigational calculations and predictions can now be conducted in a fraction of the time that was previously possible with paper charts. Additionally, the display of continuous positional and navigational information can enhance spatial awareness and decision making. However, although equipment such as Electronic Chart Display and Information Systems (ECDIS) can theoretically make navigation safer and more efficient, it is designed to ease the navigational burden rather than replace the human operator. As a result, the potential of ECDIS is very much dependent upon the skill of the watchkeeper. In this regard, very little has changed from navigating with paper charts, as ECDIS, despite its capabilities, is still only a navigational aid. This means that, although production of a safe passage plan will inevitably take less time on ECDIS than on paper charts, it still requires at least the same level of skill to compose. Additionally, the physical aspect of passage planning on such equipment presents many new challenges, despite the fact that the fundamentals of doing so remain unchanged. To overcome these obstacles, a high level of equipment knowledge is required to understand the nuances of the ECDIS software in use, as only then can its capabilities be optimised, and a safe passage plan produced.

Effective passage planning is a process that requires skill and meticulous research. It is not something that should be taken lightly, as responsibility for producing a safe passage plan brings accountability, and the consequences of getting it wrong are all too evident. A good planner must be conscientious and seek to produce a comprehensive and detailed *berth to berth* plan based upon the fullest possible appraisal, taking into account all possibilities and eventualities, whilst reducing navigational risk. An effective passage plan completed on ECDIS must fulfil all of the following criteria:

1.1 Effective Planning on ECDIS

- Clearly define the safest navigational route from berth to berth

- be comprehensive and detailed, reducing navigational risk

- take into account established safety margins

- satisfy a rigorous checking process

- be easy to follow, allowing safe execution of the plan

- be economical.

Passage planning on ECDIS is very different to using paper charts and will take time to get used to. This is mainly due to the technology being, on the whole, unintuitive and over-complicated. However, many of the frustrations and shortfalls within ECDIS can be overcome with practice and knowledge of the onboard equipment, in particular shortfalls and related workarounds. Only by understanding what the software cannot do as well as what it can do, will the underlying benefits of the system be recognised. Once proficient, planning on ECDIS can provide a faster and more efficient means of plotting passages than the paper alternative.

1.2 The Four Stages of Planning

An ECDIS voyage consists of four recognised stages:

1 Appraisal

- preliminary research
- feasibility brief.

2 Planning

- display configuration
- route creation
- supplementary information
- route check
- detailed brief.

3 Execution

- putting the plan into effect.

4 Monitoring

- charting progress in relation to the plan.

Arguably, *'Analysis'* is a fifth stage in the process, where the execution of the passage is reviewed. This provides an opportunity to discuss what was done well, what could have been done better and if anything needs to be amended to improve future voyages. This section covers the *Appraisal* and *Planning* phases of a passage when using ECDIS as the Primary Means of Navigation (PMN). The content should be used in conjunction with other, more detailed publications on ECDIS use.

1.3 Key to Symbols

Key to symbols used throughout this section:

i	**This symbol draws attention to important information.**
(!)	**This symbol draws attention to safety critical information.**
?	**This symbol highlights important changes that will come into force with edition 4.0.0 of the Presentation Library.**

2 Appraisal

Introduction

Before route construction can commence, a great deal of research is required. Although ECDIS provides efficiencies in the practical plotting of routes, it does not facilitate many of the checks, calculations and background reading required prior to commencing the physical planning. It will be necessary to undertake a feasibility study, select the best route by identifying all areas of danger and study the appropriate references before briefing the Master. This phase is called the *'Appraisal'* and comprises two steps:

- Preliminary research

- feasibility brief.

This chapter provides guidance on the preliminary calculations and checks that must be completed prior to commencing the *'Planning'* phase.

Although the navigational plan will be constructed and ultimately displayed on the ECDIS screen for the *Execution* and *Monitoring* phases, the basis for the chosen passage plan must be supported by calculations and research. There are many factors that must first be ascertained such as speed, time, distance, tide and environmental data. Such information should be documented along with supporting extracts from relevant publications. For the specific purpose of recording thought processes and background information, a workbook should be used. As soon as the ship's intended passage is known, preliminary research can begin to establish whether it is feasible within existing constraints. The following will need to be determined in order to establish whether or not the intended passage is achievable:

- Destination
  - suitability
  - distance
  - time
  - speed and endurance
- chart installation, update and review
- weather and environment
- other considerations.

The aim is to identify all areas of danger along with any difficulties and hazards associated with the passage. If early study discovers that the destination is unsuitable for the vessel or the intended passage is unachievable or dangerous, then planning time has been saved. There is a great deal of research material available in the form of paper based and digital publications for this purpose. Some ECDIS planning software can integrate with tide, current and weather databases, and provide specific tools that may aid in this process. Information is also available to the navigating officer (NO) from the relevant *Electronic Navigational Chart (ENC)* using the *'cursor pick'* function or by reviewing chart notes from any installed *Raster Navigational Charts (RNC)*. However, the cursor pick method can be time consuming and may not yield information in sufficient detail. Therefore, use of up-to-date publications issued in paper or digital format by a competent authority is recommended.

2.1 Preliminary Research

35

2.1.1 Destination

It is tempting at this stage to begin the actual construction of a route on ECDIS. However, doing so at such an early stage will raise numerous routeing and safety-related questions, all of which the *Appraisal* phase seeks to address. Planning will be quicker, more efficient and safer once the necessary facts have been established through detailed research.

a. Suitability

The suitability of the vessel with reference to the destination must be considered by taking into account constraining factors such as:

- Vessel
  - competent and well-rested crew
  - condition and state
  - draught
  - equipment
  - manoeuvring data
  - operational limitations
  - restrictions and limitations
  - stability
- cargo
  - any special characteristics (especially if hazardous)
  - distribution, stowage and securing on board
- port
  - available port information
  - restrictions and limitations (such as cargo, vessel size and draught)
  - availability of shore-based emergency response arrangements and equipment
- other
  - up-to-date certificates and documents concerning the vessel, its equipment, crew, passengers or cargo.

Consultation with the *'Manoeuvring Booklet'* and relevant *'Sailing Directions'* will help to determine whether any of the above factors affect the vessel's ability to enter port at the chosen destination. Where a manufacturer provides it, additional information regarding port entrance restrictions, facilities and services may be available in ECDIS, although unofficial information is no substitute for the relevant official and up-to-date publications (see Figures 1 and 2).

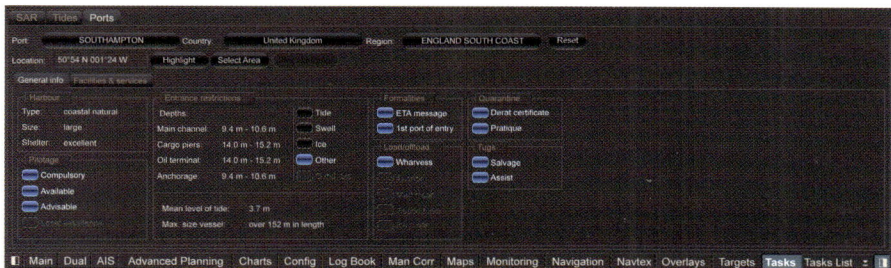

Figures 1 & 2: Some ECDIS manufacturers provide port databases that contain information such as restrictions, facilities and services (Transas)

Cursor pick is a tool that can be used to gather relevant information from the chart regarding the suitability of a vessel to a specific destination. Although it may not provide significant information, it can often point the NO towards relevant references, as in Figure 3.

Figure 3: Cursor pick may unearth additional relevant planning information (Transas)

b. Distance

The distances involved in the passage must be established. There are a number of different techniques to determine a distance between two points, such as using the *'Sailings Formula'* and tables in *'Nories'*. Another method is to use the *'Distance Tables'* to provide the shortest (Great Circle) distance between ports. If using this method, remember that the distances provided have regard to normal navigational constraints but they do not take into account ocean currents, prevailing weather conditions and Traffic Separation Schemes (TSS). Therefore, it should be used in conjunction with *'Ocean Passages for the World'*. Regardless of which method is used, it is recommended that any calculation of distance is cross checked by another means. Moreover, be sure to locate the correct geographical area as many ports have the same name. Publications such as *'Nories'* and *'Ports of the World'* contain a list of ports with their corresponding latitude and longitude for this purpose.

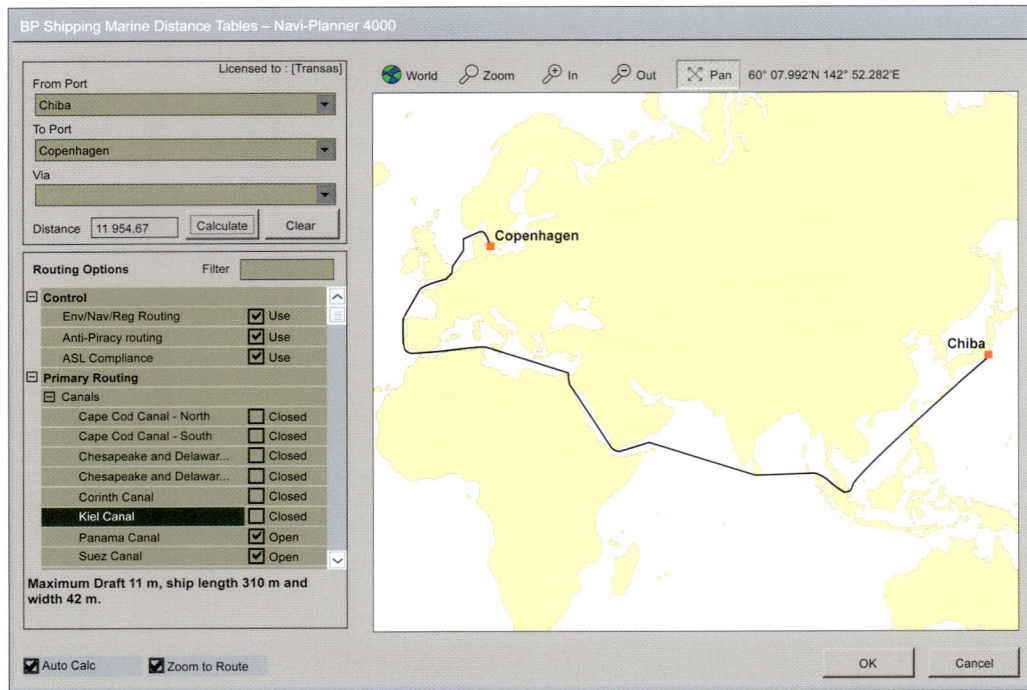

Figure 4: Example of distance table integration with ECDIS planning software that allows the automatic generation of routes (Transas)

c. Time

The amount of time available to complete the passage must be calculated to confirm that it is achievable at an economical speed. However, before this can be calculated, the time of departure and arrival must first be ascertained in case it is necessary to achieve certain tidal windows. This will depend on the required under keel clearance (UKC), tidal stream, current and port regulations, which may constrain the time of arrival and departure. Consultation with tide tables, tidal atlases and the relevant *'Sailing Directions'* will help to determine this. The following are considerations with regard to the vessel conducting the passage:

- Tidal constraints
  - high water (HW), low water (LW), height of tide (HoT), % springs
  - draught in relation to HoT, squat and required UKC
  - vertical clearances

- times of strong tidal stream and current
- port regulations and restrictions
  - draught permissible in fairway and port
  - restrictions with regard to port sailing times
  - pilot availability.

When calculating the amount of safe water required to leave and enter harbour safely, then the equation for *Safety Depth* in Figure 5 may be used. This will provide a least depth value that will be entered in ECDIS prior to undertaking route construction.

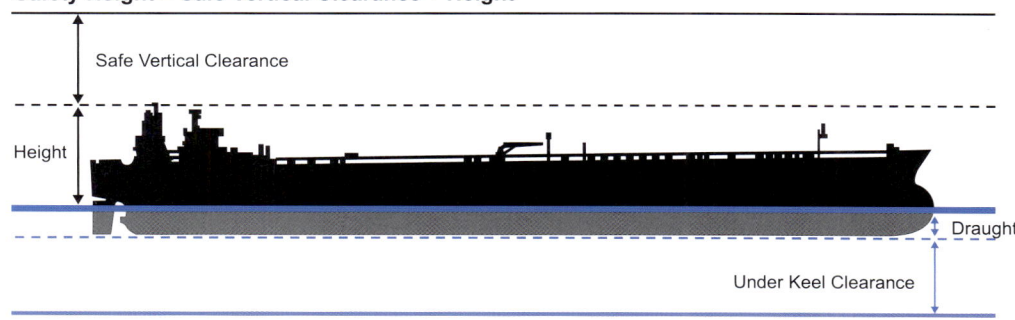

Safety Height = Safe Vertical Clearance + Height

Safety Contour = Draught + Under Keel Clearance (inc squat and a safety margin) – Height of Tide

Figure 5: The calculation of the safety contour will be used to define safe navigable water (MJI)

 **Although horizontal datum within ENCs is standardised to WGS84, vertical datums may differ between chart producers.**

Tidal calculation software is widely available as an alternative to the traditional paper tide tables and tidal atlases. Such products may be capable of integration with ECDIS or be used as a stand-alone application (see Figures 6 and 7).

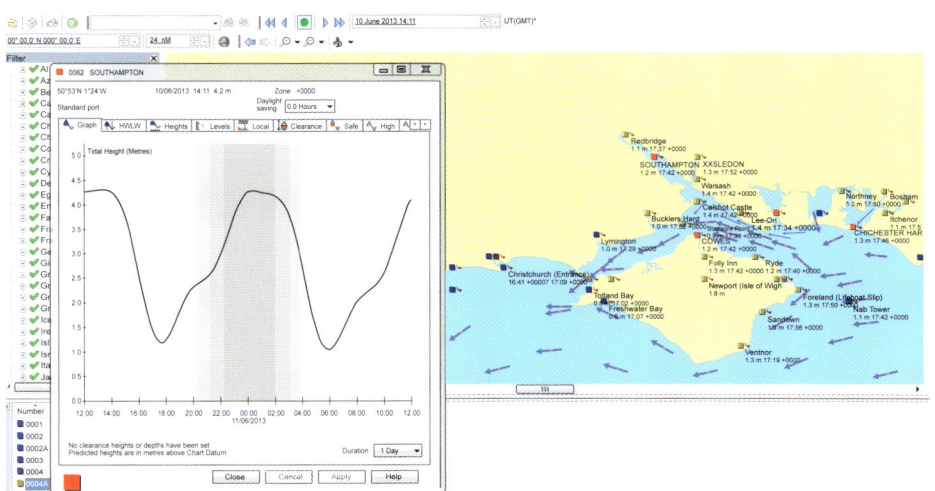

Figure 6: Official tidal databases such as 'Admiralty Total Tide' (ATT) can be integrated with ECDIS to assist with tide and current predictions and for calculating times of astronomical events (UKHO)

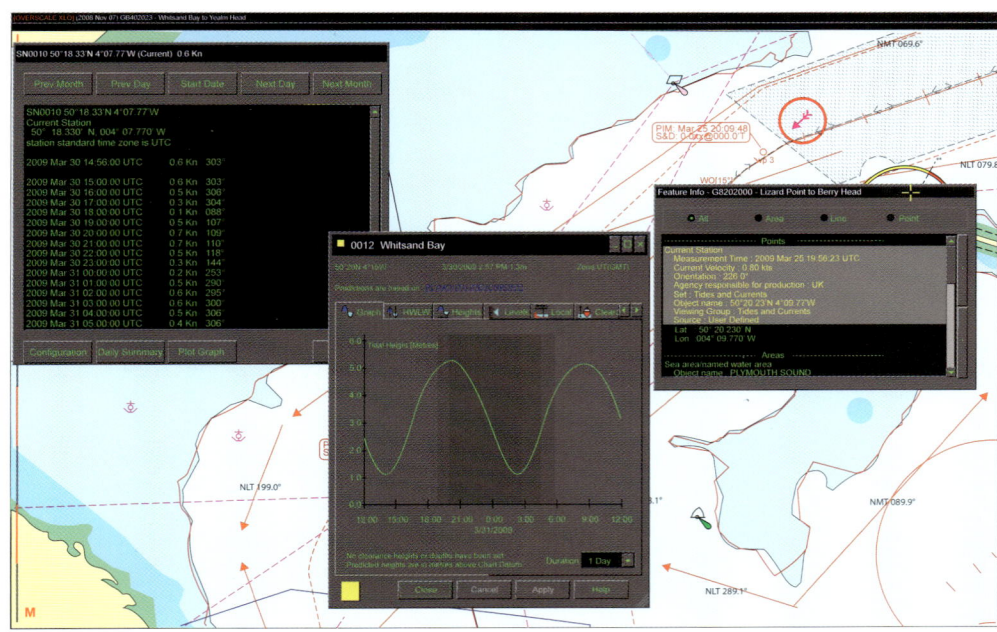

Figure 7: An example of ATT integrated with ECDIS (OSI)

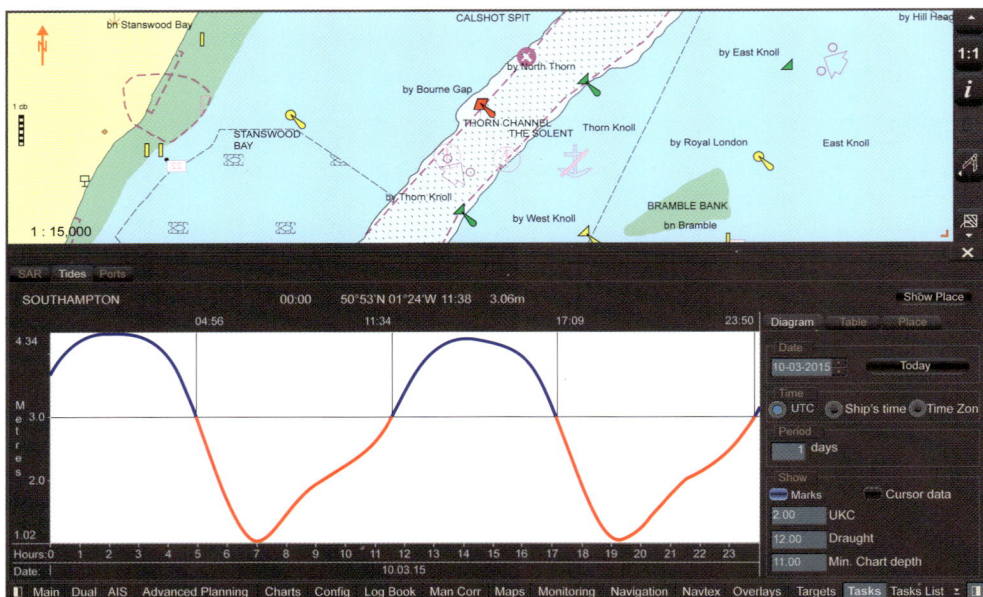

Figure 8: An example of a tidal database provided by the ECDIS manufacturer (Transas)

The calculations resulting from this research should identify relevant tidal windows and provide an estimated time of departure (ETD) and arrival (ETA).

 Be aware when using databases provided by ECDIS manufacturers, particularly tidal databases, as they may not be official or endorsed by flag State, even when data is extracted from official sources. Additionally, not all flag States recognise digital nautical publications as satisfying carriage requirements, even where such data is available in official digital format.

d. Speed and Endurance

The overall speed required to achieve the ETA can now be resolved. Consider whether any of the following will hamper achieving and maintaining this calculated speed:

- Speed constraints
    - economical speed range
    - environmental factors
    - limits and restrictions
    - machinery limitations and defects
- endurance constraints
    - bunker capacity
    - fuel economy
    - minimum reserve of fuel
    - refuelling opportunities
    - stability.

 **If, by this stage, factors that make the passage unfeasible have been identified, then these must be brought to the attention of the Master at the earliest opportunity.**

2.1.2 Weather and Environment

The weather and any environmental factors likely to affect the passage must now be determined. It will be necessary to gather climatological, meteorological and oceanographic data to estimate the likely statistical weather for the passage. *'Routeing Charts'*, *'Routeing Guides'* and *'Sailing Directions'* published by competent authorities should be consulted for this purpose. The following factors should be considered:

- Likely statistical weather conditions
    - mean pressure
    - mean temperature
    - precipitation
    - visibility and probability of fog
    - wave height
    - wind strength
        - o hurricane season
        - o tropical storms
- likely statistical environmental conditions
    - ice limits
    - ocean currents.

In addition to paper publications, some ECDIS can integrate with weather routeing services. Where this capability exists, it may be necessary to construct a route in ECDIS. If so, an approximate route is all that is required at this stage.

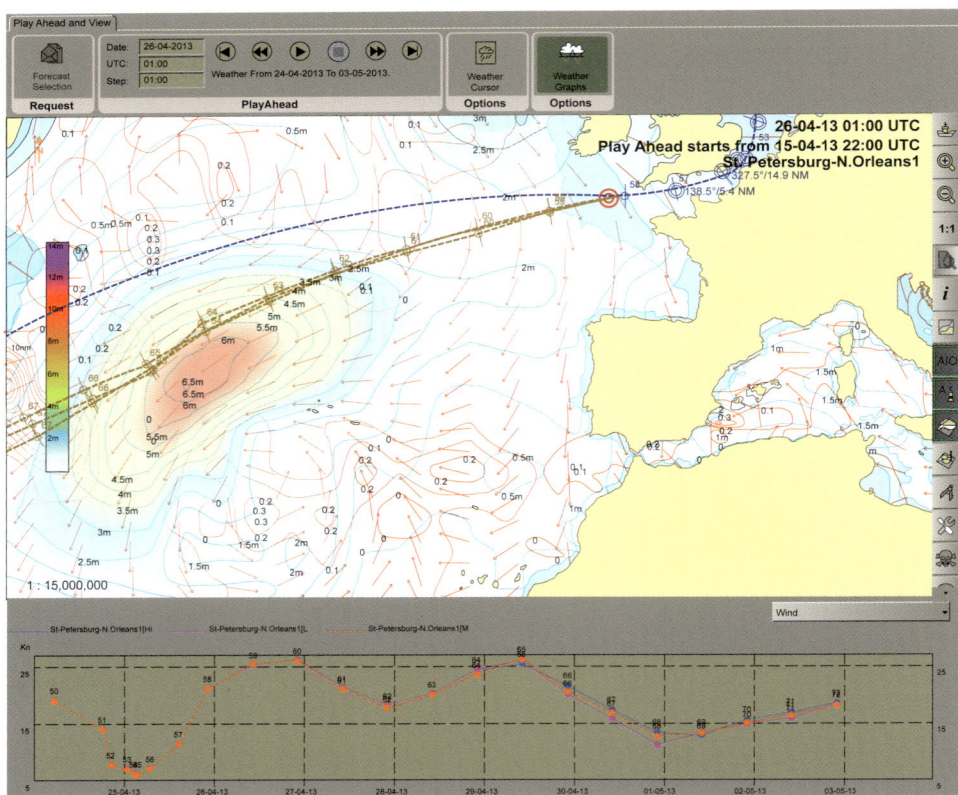

Figures 9 & 10: Some ECDIS passage planning software facilitates the simulation of likely weather conditions, allowing optimal routes that avoid weather patterns to be identified (Transas)

It is also possible to use ECDIS to display chart products that can help ascertain the existence or extent of ice. This is particularly important when planning to use a great circle route at high or low latitudes and when planning to travel through or near areas that are prone to ice formation (see Figures 11 and 12).

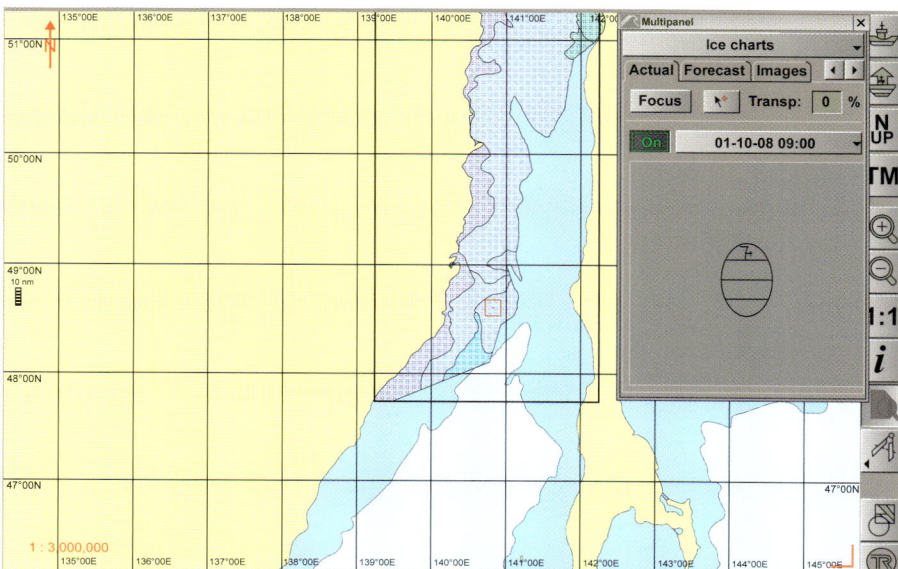

Figure 11: An example of an ice chart overlay (Transas)

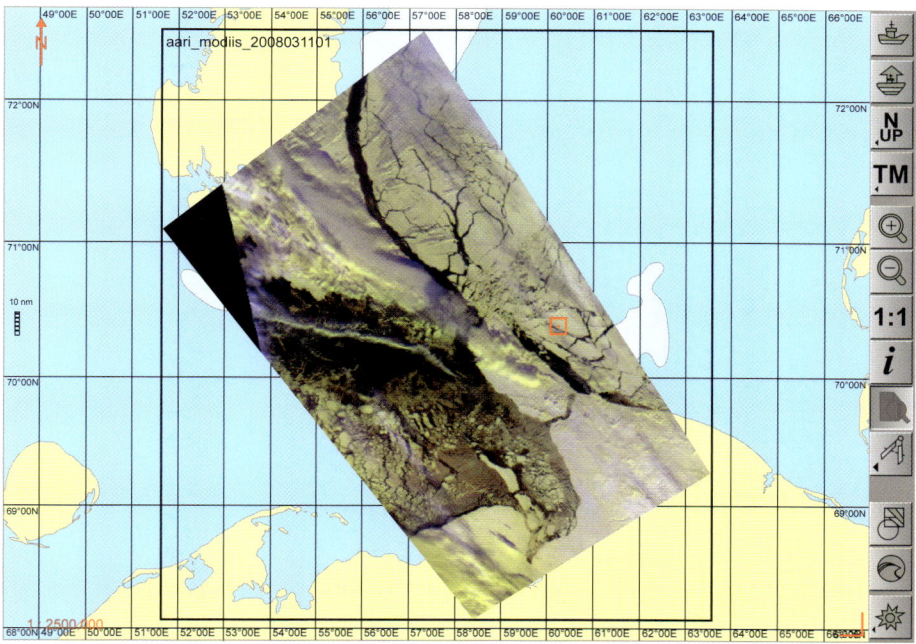

Figure 12: A satellite image that can be used to show ice formation relative to land mass (Transas)

 The IHO has a working group that is currently investigating the possibility of incorporating ice information within the ENC format.

2.1.3   Chart Installation, Update and Review

The likely routes should now start to present themselves. The next stage is to ensure that ECDIS has charts of an appropriate scale and format installed for the planning phase, that they are up to date and have been reviewed for content and accuracy. In order to meet SOLAS carriage requirements, electronic charts used in ECDIS must be official, meaning they must be issued by or on authority of a Government, authorised Hydrographic Office (HO) or other relevant government institution and conform to IHO standards. ENCs and RNCs are the only official formats sanctioned by the IMO for use in ECDIS, when used as the PMN. If there are insufficient ENCs of an appropriate scale to cover the entire route, then RNCs may be used to fill any gaps.

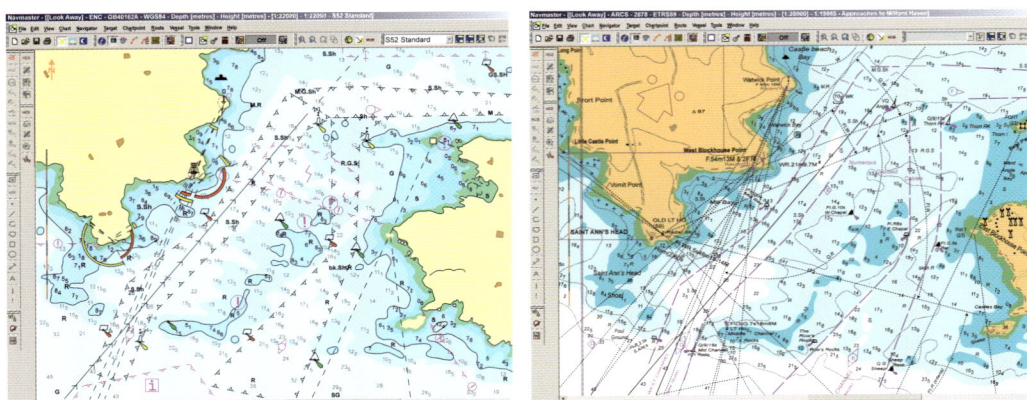

Figures 13 & 14: Example of an ENC (left) and equivalent scale RNC (right) for the same area (PC Maritime)

An RNC is essentially a scan of a paper chart, and when used in ECDIS the system is in *Raster Chart Display System* (RCDS) mode. As RCDS mode does not have the full functionality of ECDIS due to the limitations of the format, particularly with regard to scaling and availability of overview, RNCs must be used in conjunction with an appropriate portfolio of official, up-to-date paper charts (APC). Assuming the ECDIS fitted on board is type-approved, Figure 15 can be used to ascertain whether a chart outfit is SOLAS compliant.

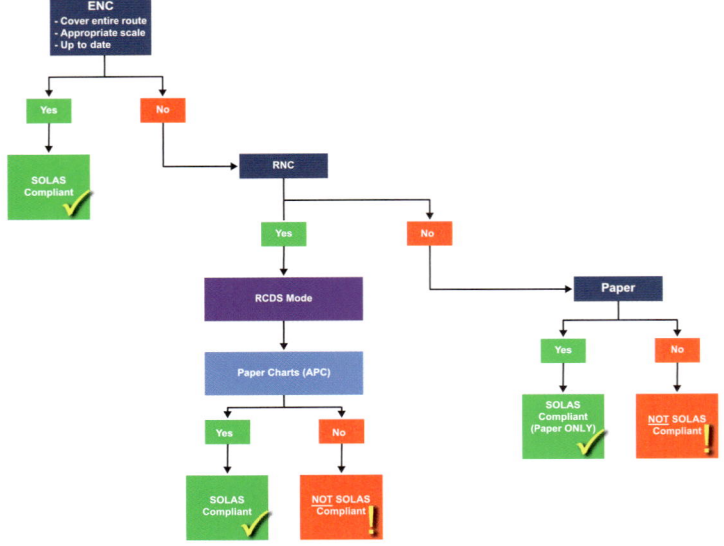

Figure 15: SOLAS chart compliancy diagram (MJI)

The required content of the APC varies between flag States. The relevant authority should be consulted where doubt exists.

The diagram in Figure 15 only refers to official data formats permitted for use in ECDIS, and the reversion to official paper charts where these do not exist. Although unofficial chart data may be used in ECDIS as a supplementary aid to navigation, such data does not meet SOLAS chart carriage requirements when ECDIS is used as the PMN.

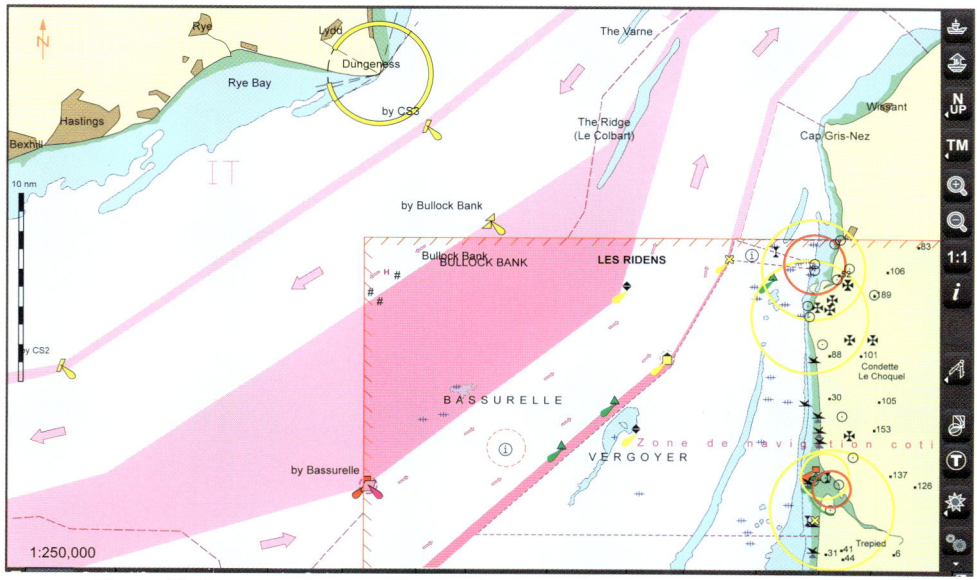

Figure 16: An example of unofficial TX-97 data, produced to the S-57 standard, fused with an ENC (Transas)

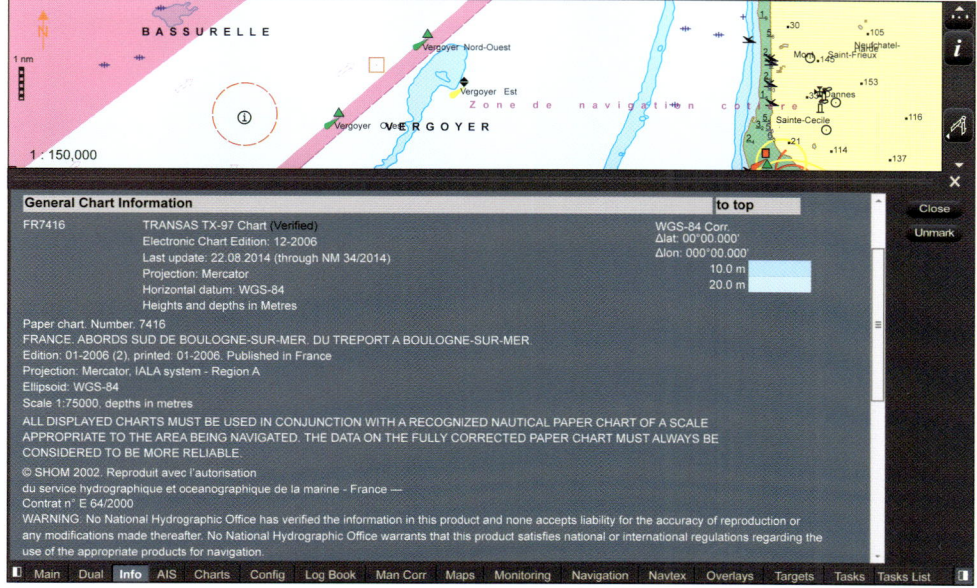

Figure 17: Cursor pick information from a TX-97 chart showing associated warning message that such data should be used in conjunction with official paper charts (Transas)

If an IMO-compliant ECDIS is using unofficial chart data for navigation, the ECDIS is classified as an electronic chart system (ECS) only and cannot be used as the PMN.

Identifying any shortfalls in the chart outfit at an early stage is crucial to the success of the plan, given that planning cannot be completed without the relevant charts first being installed in ECDIS. If the requisite charts are not already installed, then additional charts will need to be sourced. The relevant official digital chart catalogue can be consulted in order to establish what charts are required. Where a route is required to be inserted, an approximation will suffice.

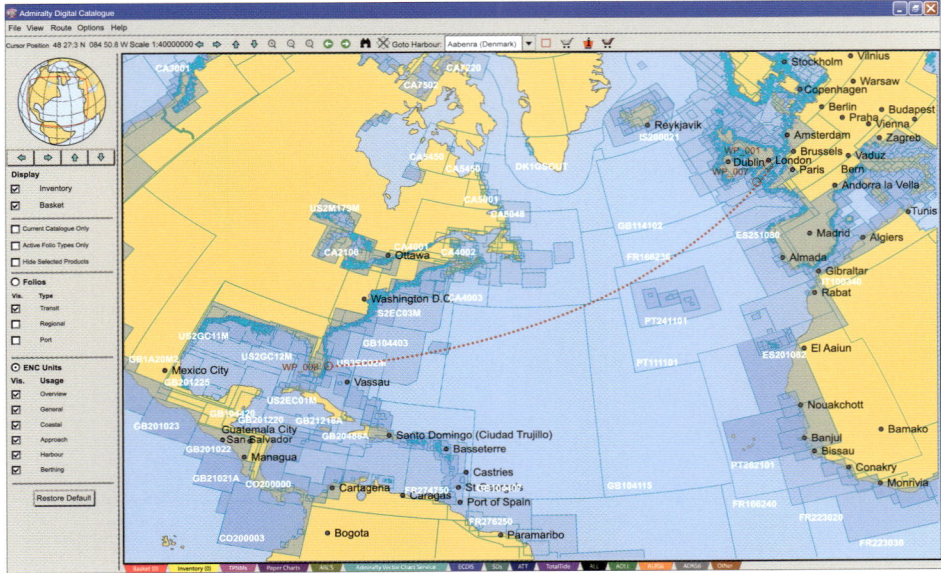

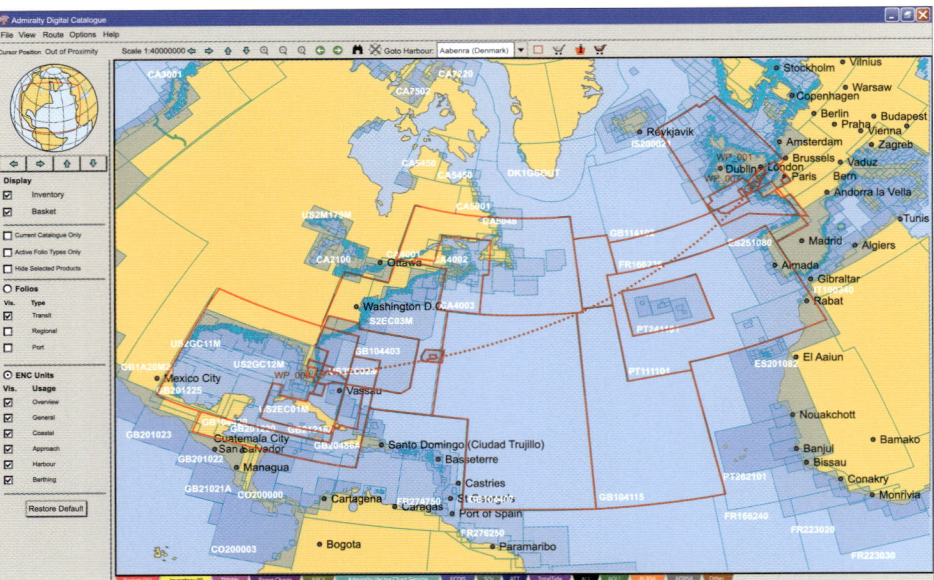

Figures 18 & 19: Products like the Admiralty Digital Catalogue (available online from the UKHO) can be used to identify and purchase appropriate charts in a variety of formats (UKHO)

Chart catalogues, such as the Admiralty Digital Catalogue, are invaluable for quickly identifying the quantities and formats of charts required for any given route. Gaps in ENC coverage or areas where insufficient ENCs of an appropriate scale exist can be identified, allowing RNCs, paper charts and relevant publications to be sourced. In Figure 19, relevant charts are highlighted in red where they intersect with the route. Additionally, a *'buffer width'* either side of the route can be added to cater for route adjustment during the planning phase, and to cover contingency.

a. Chart Installation and Update

Once the necessary charts have been identified and sourced, they will need to be installed and updated in ECDIS prior to being reviewed. The following are considerations when installing and updating chart data:

- Chart installation
    - permits and licence
        o relevant ENC and RNC permits held
        o permits are up to date (will individual permits expire during the voyage?)
        o ECDIS subscription expiry (will it expire during the voyage?)
    - relevant base discs are held on board
    - the length of time it takes to procure and receive chart data
    - the length of time it takes to install chart data in ECDIS
- chart updates
    - charts are up to date on all ECDIS to the latest:
        o notice to mariners (NM) (note that the IHO abbreviates this as NM and not NTM)
        o temporary and preliminary notices to mariners (T&P)
        o local NM
        o radio navigational warnings (NAVAREAS)
    - the latest NM update is held on board
    - use of the admiralty information overlay (AIO)
    - the length of time it takes to update chart data in ECDIS.

It must be appreciated that chart installation and update times can be considerable. Recording the time it takes to complete this process will allow more accurate estimates to be used in future.

Failure to renew chart subscriptions will result in a permanent warning message whenever an expired cell is displayed, stating that the cell may be out of date and must not be used for primary navigation. Moreover, it will not be possible to update expired cells with official updates until the subscription has been renewed, during which time the vessel will be in direct contravention of the chart carriage requirements.

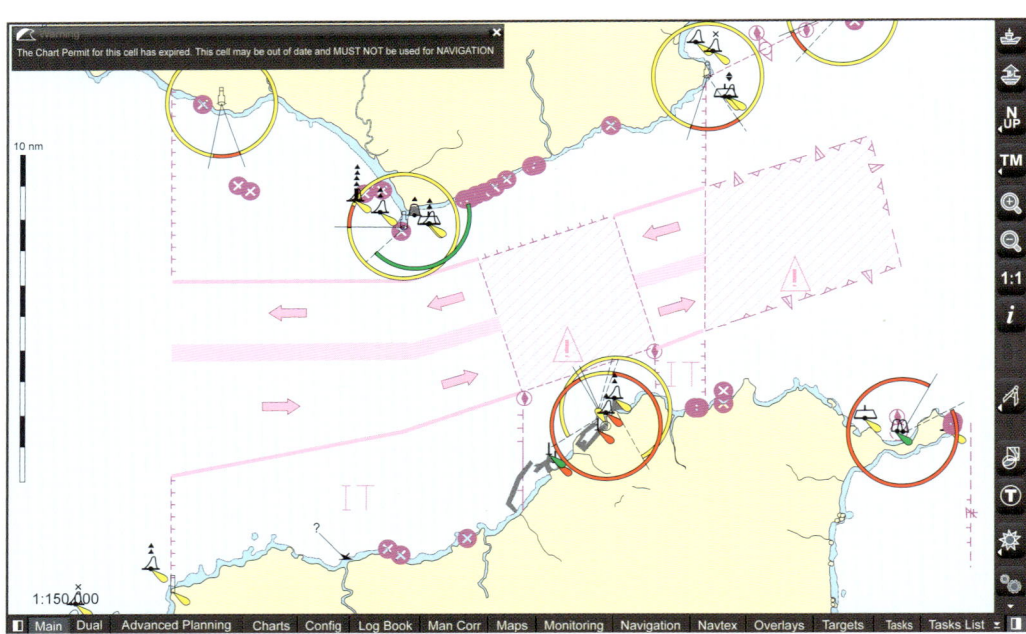

Figure 20: It is important to competently manage chart subscriptions and permits to ensure that they do not expire during the passage (Transas)

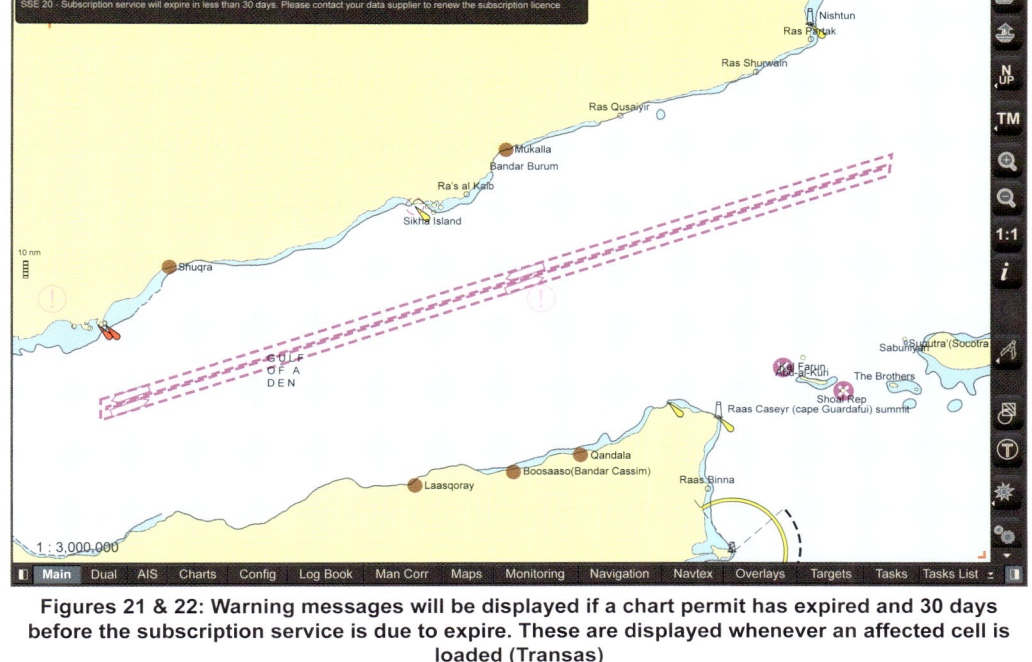

Figures 21 & 22: Warning messages will be displayed if a chart permit has expired and 30 days before the subscription service is due to expire. These are displayed whenever an affected cell is loaded (Transas)

Chart installation and updating can be a frustrating process, particularly when installing encrypted data, or when errors are encountered (see EP Annex A S-63 Error Codes and Explanations). When installing encrypted data from chart providers that are signatories to the IHO *S-63 Data Protection Scheme*, it's important that ECDIS software is up to date to ensure compatibility with the latest edition. It is also important to ensure that the correct scheme administrator (SA) and chart producer certificates are installed to facilitate chart installation (see EP section 2.1.2 Chart Installation). Sufficient knowledge of the process and the specific ECDIS in use is an essential prerequisite for successful chart installation and the avoidance of timely delays.

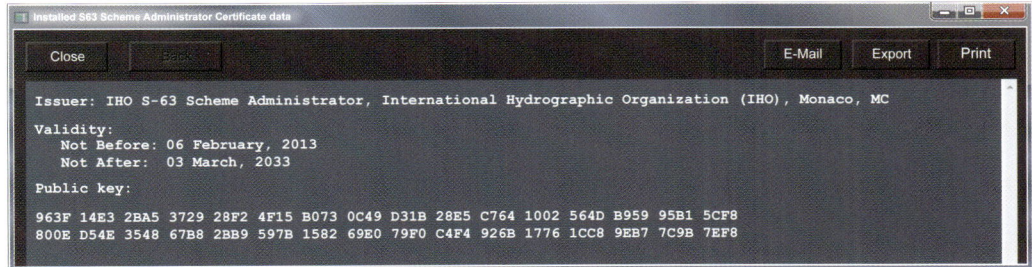

Figure 23: Encrypted ENCs can make installing and updating charts a frustrating process if an operator does not understand the IHO S-63 Data Protection Scheme (Transas)

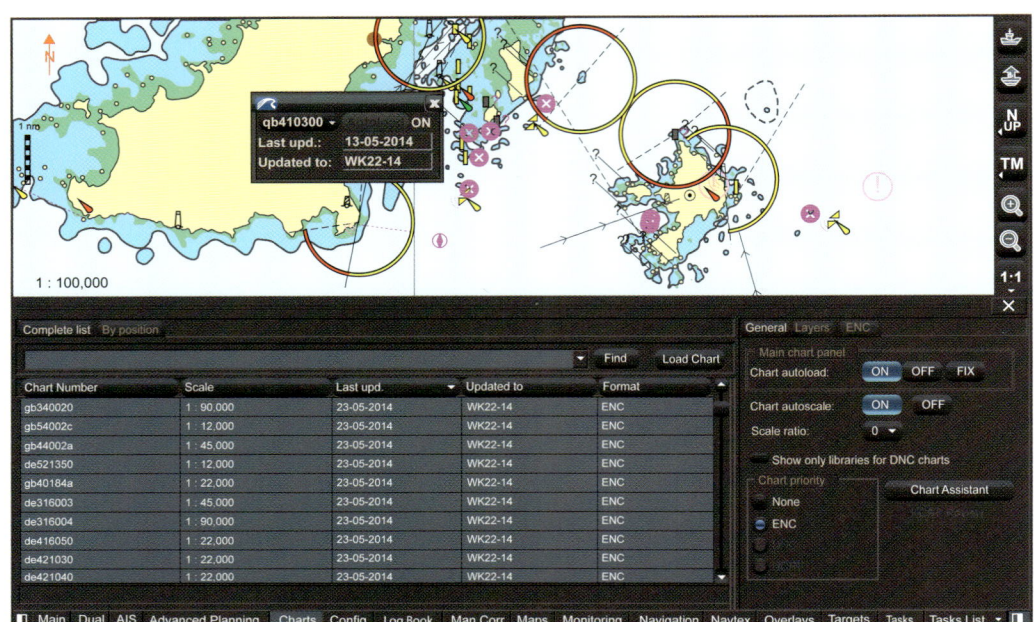

Figure 24: The date and number of the latest update affecting chart cells in use should be available (Transas)

b. Chart Review

A review of installed data should be undertaken to identify its accuracy, that it is of an appropriate scale, and that there are no gaps in coverage. The following are considerations when reviewing chart data:

- Official chart formats
  - the entire route is covered by ENCs of an appropriate scale and accuracy:
    - o areas of ENC overlap are identified
    - o areas of low chart accuracy are identified
    - o areas of no known datum are identified
    - o areas of poor GNSS coverage are identified
  - where ECDIS supports RCDS mode:
    - o the relevant flag State permits RCDS mode
    - o gaps in ENC coverage are filled by appropriate scale RNCs
    - o an appropriate portfolio of paper charts is available
    - o RCDS mode risk assessment is conducted
  - where ECDIS does not support RCDS mode:
    - o gaps in ENC coverage are filled by appropriate scale paper charts
  - sufficient chart provision in case of diversion and contingency.

When conducting the review, the NO should have visibility of installed ENC data, allowing him to see whether better scale charts are available and spot gaps in coverage (see Figure 25). This function may also be useful during route construction. The six available *'navigational purpose bands'* are shown in section 3.2.1 New Route.

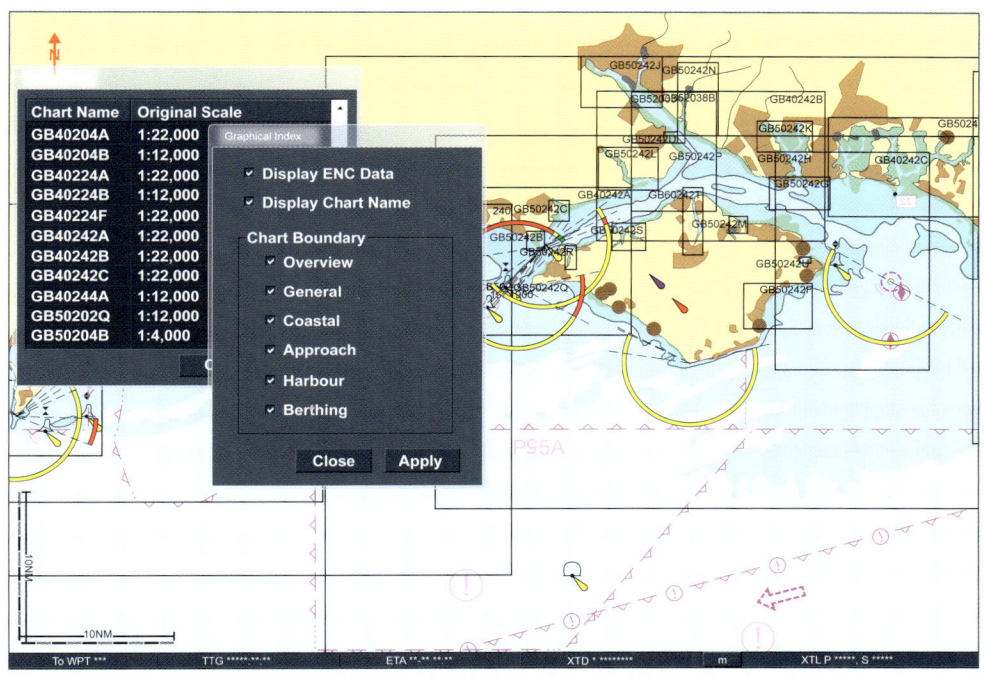

Figure 25: An example of a graphical index, classified by navigational purpose, of all installed ENC data (JRC)

When reviewing the accuracy of installed data, it should be noted that ENCs do not contain a *Source Data Diagram* as depicted on paper charts. Instead, the quality of survey data is displayed using *'Category of Zone of Confidence in data'*, or *CATZOC* for short. The understanding of these symbols is critical to interpreting the accuracy of presented survey data. Explanations of the six CATZOC symbols are provided in Figure 26.

1	2	3		4	5	6
ZOC	Position Accuracy	Depth Accuracy		Seafloor Coverage	Typical Survey Characteristics	Symbol
A1	± 5 m	= 0.50 + 1%d		Full area search undertaken. All significant seafloor features detected and depths measured.	Controlled, systematic survey, high position and depth accuracy achieved using DGPS or a minimum three high quality lines of position (LOP) and a multibeam, channel or mechanical sweep system.	✶ ✶ ✶ ✶ ✶ ✶
		Depth (m)	Accuracy (m)			
		10 30 100 1000	± 0.6 ± 0.8 ± 1.5 ± 10.5			
A2	± 20 m	= 1.00 + 2%d		Full area search undertaken. All significant seafloor features detected and depths measured.	Controlled, systematic survey achieving position and depth accuracy less than ZOC A1 and using a modern survey echosounder and a sonar or mechanical sweep system.	✶ ✶ ✶ ✶ ✶
		Depth (m)	Accuracy (m)			
		10 30 100 1000	± 1.2 ± 1.6 ± 3.0 ± 21.0			
B	± 50 m	= 1.00 + 2%d		Full area search not achieved; uncharted features, hazardous to surface navigation are not expected but may exist.	Controlled, systematic survey achieving similar depth but lesser position accuracies than ZOC A2, using a modern survey echosounder, but no sonar or mechanical sweep system.	✶ ✶ ✶ ✶
		Depth (m)	Accuracy (m)			
		10 30 100 1000	± 1.2 ± 1.6 ± 3.0 ± 21.0			
C	± 500 m	= 2.00 + 5%d		Full area search not achieved, depth anomalies may be expected.	Low accuracy survey or data collected on an opportunity basis such as soundings on passage.	✶ ✶ ✶
		Depth (m)	Accuracy (m)			
		10 30 100 1000	± 2.5 ± 3.5 ± 7.0 ± 52.0			
D	worse than ZOC C	Worse Than ZOC C		Full area search not achieved, large depth anomalies may be expected.	Poor quality data or data that cannot be quality assessed due to lack of information.	✶ ✶
U	Unassessed – The quality of the bathymetric data has yet to be assessed					U

Figure 26: CATZOCs provide an indication of ENC accuracy (IHO)

Despite huge advances in hydrographic technology, many ENCs are derived from the source data of the equivalent paper chart, and are no more accurate as a result. NOs must be mindful that there is always potential for error and the presence of undetected dangers, despite the most conscientious of chart reviews.

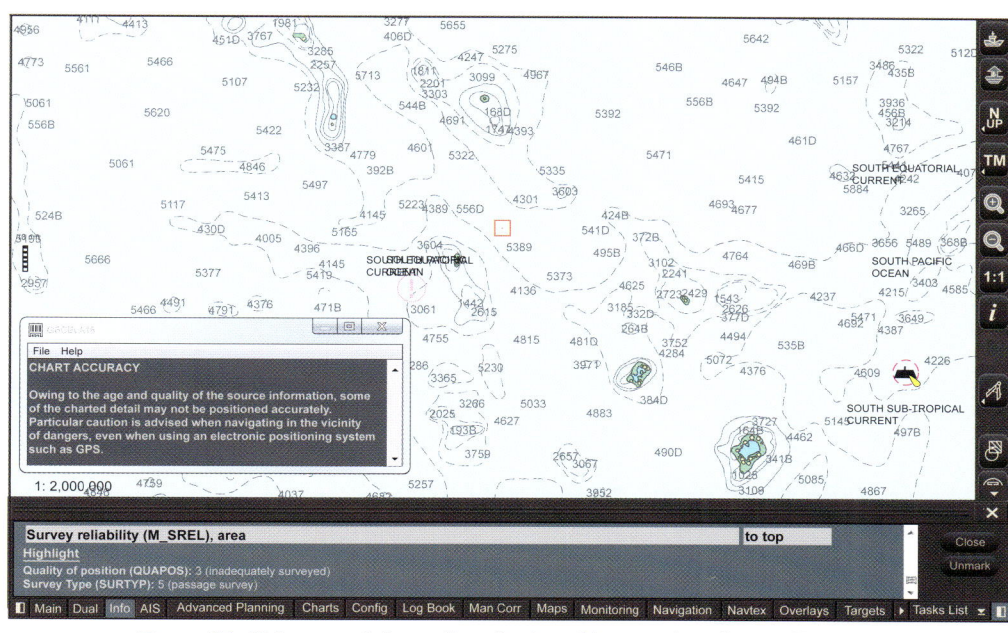

Figure 27: Old source information displayed in a modern format (Transas)

Figure 28: Many ENCs are no more accurate than the equivalent paper chart, and are constantly being corrected as new information comes to light (Transas)

? The operator must be able to display automatic chart corrections made to the SENC, on demand.

2.1.4 Other Considerations

The final stage of preliminary research is to consider any additional factors that may influence the route before actual planning can commence. As a minimum, the following should be given due consideration:

- Routeing
    - anchorage(s)
    - areas to be avoided
    - bridge manning
    - canals
    - danger areas
    - day or night transit of critical points
    - deep water (DW) routes
    - environmental protection
        - o emission control areas (ECA)
        - o *'International Convention for the Prevention of Pollution from Ships'* (MARPOL)
        - o marine environmental protection measures/particularly sensitive sea areas (PSSA)
    - IALA buoyage systems
    - load lines
    - military/naval weapon practice areas
    - NAVAID coverage
    - pilotage embarkation, disembarkation and exchange of information
    - piracy
    - precautionary areas
    - shipping lanes
    - territorial waters
    - time zones and time zone changes
    - traffic density and likely concentrations of fishing vessels
    - traffic separation schemes (TSS)
    - vessel traffic services and ship reporting systems (VTS)
- delays
    - likelihood of a change in orders
    - operations such as gas freeing, purging, cargo grade change, ballast water exchange
- ECDIS
    - adequate generic and type-specific training completed
    - latest software installed.

This list is not exhaustive and will depend upon the type of vessel and geographic area through which the passage is planned. For example, piracy is localised to specific areas of the world, and becomes a concern when transiting areas such as the Gulf of Aden, Malacca Straits and Indian Ocean. However, there are numerous sources of information available to aid the planner, some of which is available within ECDIS passage planning software (see Figure 29).

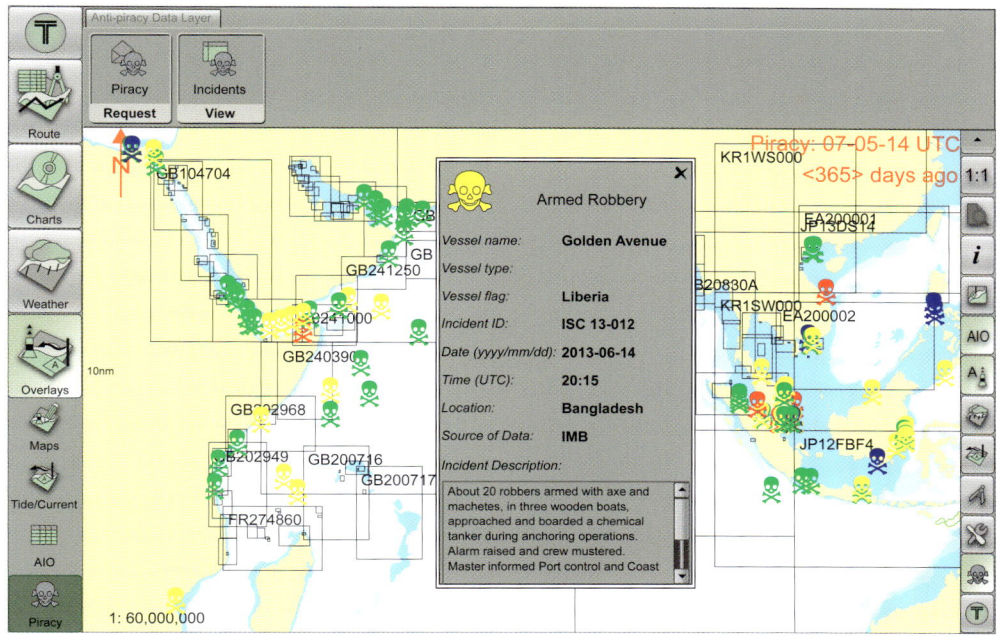

Figure 29: Anti-piracy databases are useful when considering the risk of viable routes (Transas)

Critical to the success of the planning phase and safe execution of the route is that all operators have received adequate, approved generic ECDIS training, and have also undertaken type-specific training in order to operate the specific equipment fitted on board. It is also essential for the safety of navigation that the manufacturer's software within ECDIS works fully in accordance with the latest IHO presentation library (PL) and data protection standards. Only then will ECDIS be capable of displaying all the relevant digital information contained within the ENC. Ultimately, failure to update the software may mean the ECDIS fitted on board does not meet the carriage requirements set out in SOLAS, and may result in the following equipment shortfalls:

- Navigationally significant features are not displayed

- appropriate alarms and indications may not be activated

- the latest charted features, such as Archipelagic Sea Lanes (ASL) or PSSAs, are not displayed

- ENCs may fail to install or load.

It will be necessary for the NO to know the state of software update, although this information should also be available within the system.

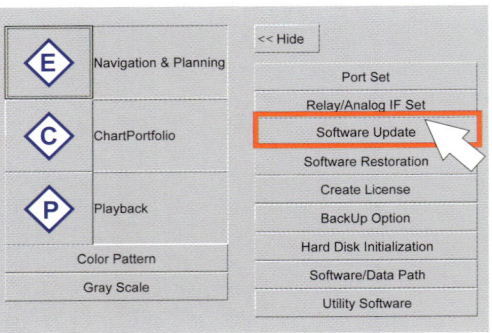

Figure 30: The importance of updating ECDIS software cannot be overemphasised. Manufacturers will normally provide instructions on how to perform the update (JRC)

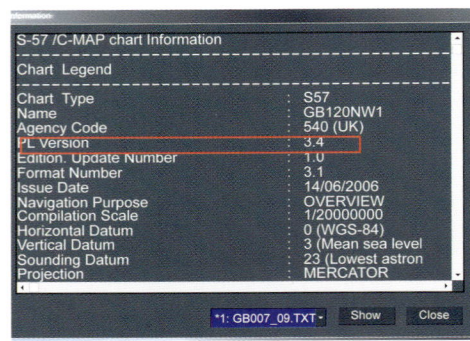

Figure 31: The version of the Presentation Library installed should be readily available to the operator. Here, it is stated in the chart legend within the pick report (JRC)

As with all software, there will always be glitches. Known anomalies within ECDIS are usually rectified by the manufacturer with software patches. It is, therefore, important that the latest patch is installed in ECDIS and that the most recent IMO guidance on ECDIS anomalies has been read. Moreover, any anomalies encountered during use should be fed back to the appropriate authority.

 **All potential hazards and dangers identified during the appraisal should be noted for reference during the Planning phase.**

2.2 Feasibility Brief

A thorough overall appraisal of the intended voyage should now have been completed, and relevant information documented. Armed with all the facts from the fullest possible appraisal, the ship's Master now needs to be briefed about the passage in order to gain approval prior to the commencement of the physical planning. This briefing will also provide a convenient opportunity for the Master to make any inputs with regard to the intended plan. The brief should cover all relevant information obtained during the research.

3   Planning

Introduction

Once the briefing is complete and the passage concepts have been approved by the Master, detailed planning can take place. The *Planning* phase is made up of five stages:

- Display configuration

- route creation

- supplementary information

- route check

- detailed brief.

ECDIS facilitates faster passage planning when compared to using paper charts, but the advantages can only be fully exploited if databases containing relevant information for planning are integrated within ECDIS passage planning software. The availability of digital resources in a single application allows relevant information to be displayed whilst the plan is being constructed. Ultimately, this not only makes planning a less onerous and time consuming task, but reduces the potential to miss important information or steps in the planning process. Although progress has been made in this field, not all ECDIS can integrate with digital publications or additional databases.

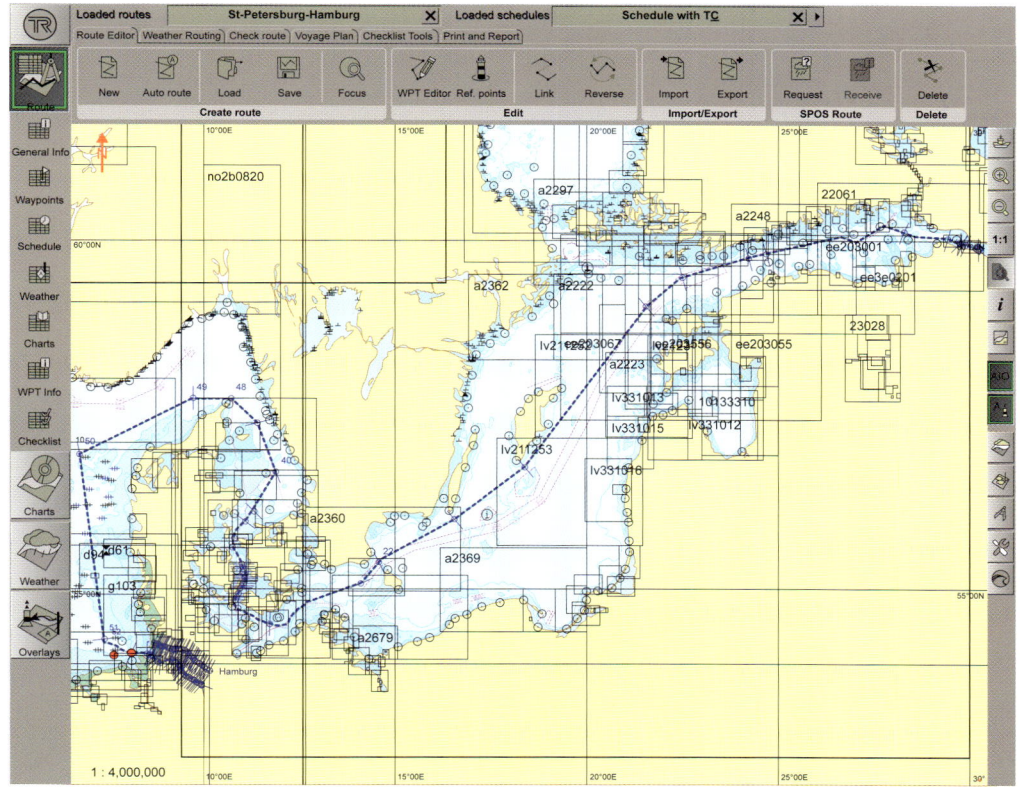

Figure 32: Some ECDIS passage planning software can facilitate multiple planning functions within a single application, including access to weather forecasts, distance tables and tidal databases, making passage planning a less onerous task (Transas)

ECDIS can be utilised for passage planning whilst alongside. However, a planning terminal or additional ECDIS console will be required if planning while underway, in order that planning does not interfere with navigation.

 **Passage planning while route monitoring on ECDIS should be avoided. As well as interfering with the ship's navigation, it can cause safety parameters to be altered, and as a result is an inherently dangerous practice.**

3.1 Display Configuration

Unlike a paper chart that contains a specific level of detail, ENCs provide a layering of information, much of which can be turned on or off by selecting the relevant display category or by using switches called *'Independent Mariner Selectors'*. In order that all relevant information for planning the passage is shown, display settings must be configured prior to constructing the route.

a. Chart Settings

Firstly, it is necessary to configure chart settings to allow fast, efficient planning to take place. The following are considerations when doing so:

- Chart settings
  - unload all routes
  - unload all mariner's notes and *mariner's navigational objects*
  - select full screen by hiding the sidebar
  - select day white palette
  - select ENC as chart priority
  - allow automatic chart loading
  - allow automatic chart scaling.

Unloading all routes and supplementary information and selecting full screen, where available, will provide the planner with as large a blank canvas to work with as is possible. Chart settings such as chart autoload, autoscale and priority, or equivalent functions, should be optimised to facilitate the efficient automatic loading of charts in the chosen format, at their respective compilation scales, in the cursor position and when zooming.

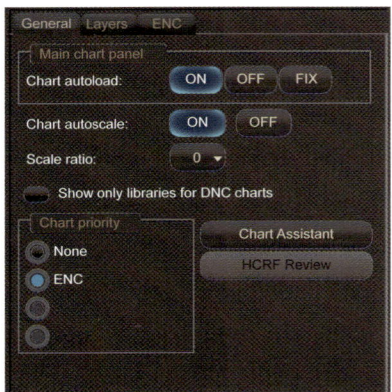

Figure 33: Configuration of ECDIS for route planning should allow optimal loading and scaling of charts in the cursor position and when zooming (Transas)

b. Safety Contour

Next, the availability of safe navigable water upon which the passage may be planned must be established. This is achieved using the *Safety Contour* function. Values for the safety contour calculated during the appraisal should now be entered into ECDIS. Figure 34 shows the delineation of safe water and unsafe water following the application of a safety contour value of 10 m. The safety contour is represented by a bold grey contour line, the area beyond which is unsafe water; safe water is represented by the white area. The bold soundings, displayed when soundings are selected for display, represent soundings equal to or less than the *Safety Depth* value.

 **Note that it is possible on some systems to set the safety contour value as 0 m. It is also possible to set the safety depth as a larger value than the safety contour. Values should be carefully entered and checked to ensure that the correct values are set prior to the commencement of planning.**

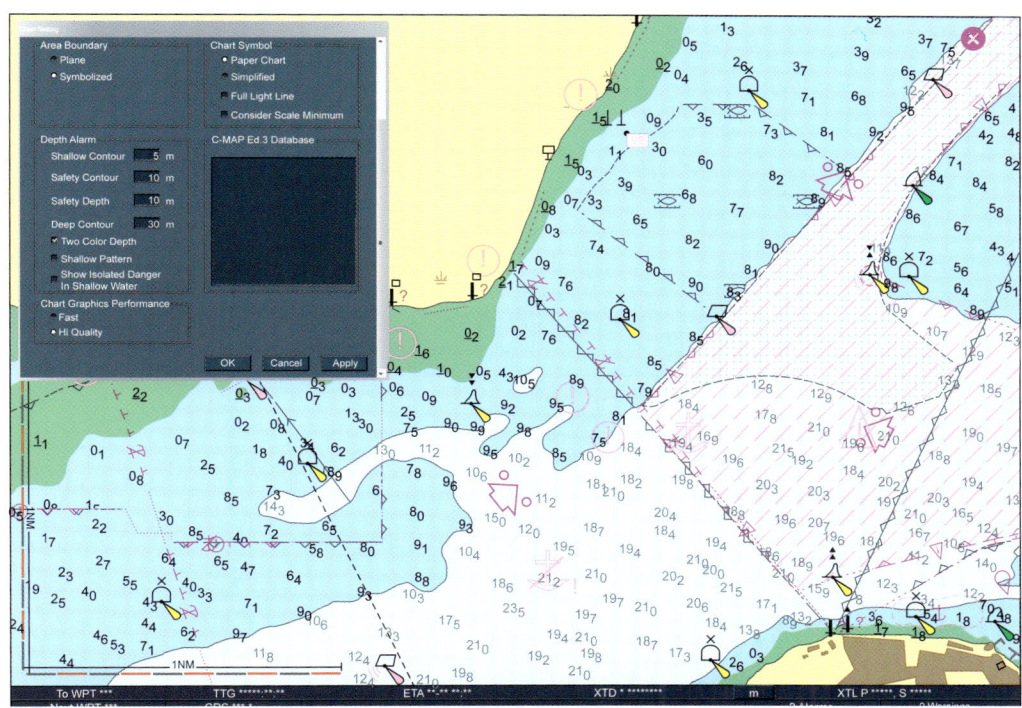

Figure 34: The ability to provide delineation between safe and unsafe water using the safety contour is a major advantage of ECDIS over paper charts (JRC)

The need for a safety depth value is born of a lack of synchronisation between the desired safety contour value and the availability of depth contours within the SENC. The symmetry in Figure 34 is only possible when the safety contour value desired is the same as that displayed, due to a depth contour equal to this value being available within the SENC. In Figure 35, the desired safety contour value is different from that displayed. The NO has calculated that the least depth for safe navigation is 7 m, but this contour does not exist within the SENC. Consequently, the next available deeper contour, the 10 m contour in this case, has been automatically selected for display instead. In such circumstances, it is prudent to enter a safety depth value equal to the calculated safety contour value, as the bold soundings represent the actual limits of safe water. This is particularly important where differences between calculated and displayed safety contour values make it necessary to plan to cross the safety contour, such as when entering or leaving port (see EP Section 2.1.9 Safety Contour). Where this is the case, it must be carefully planned and annotated.

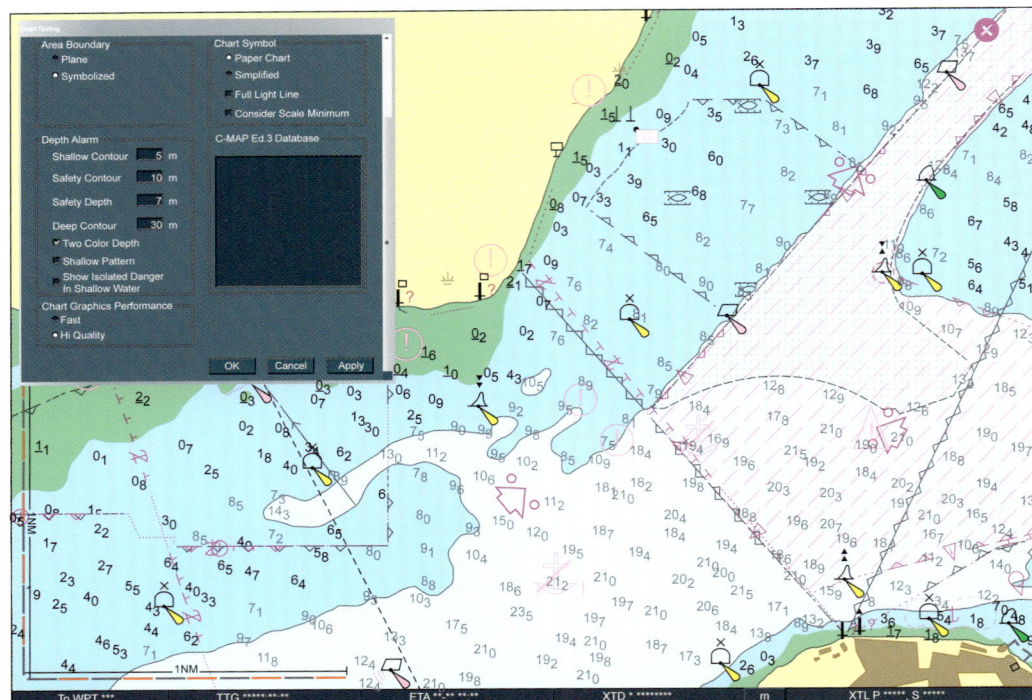

Figure 35: Where the calculated safety contour value differs from that displayed, it does not represent the actual limits of safe water (JRC)

It should be noted that only one safety contour may be displayed in ECDIS at any one time. If it is the intention to change the value of the safety contour during the passage, then consideration should be given to how this can be managed safely. One option is to use a worst case value for the entire route, whilst another is to use more than one planned route (see 3.2.4 Multiple Routes).

 **Where the calculated safety contour value cannot be displayed, it is recommended that this value be highlighted using the safety depth function. Doing so means that the actual limit of safe water will be shown when soundings are selected for display.**

 **Although some ENCs contain depth contour values expressed as decimals, not all ECDIS allow decimal values for safety contour or safety depth to be entered.**

The safety contour value also determines the display of the isolated underwater danger symbol [SY(ISODGR01)]. As a result, any difference between the calculated value and that chosen for display may mean that isolated underwater dangers may not be hazardous to navigation. For example, in Figure 36, the safety contour value calculated by the NO is 7 m, but this contour does not exist in the SENC and so the displayed safety contour value is 10 m, it being the next deepest available contour. The isolated danger selected for pick report has a sounding value of 9.1 m. Given that there is a 2.1 m difference between the calculated least depth and that displayed, this isolated danger is not a danger to navigation, although prudence may dictate that it is still best to avoid it.

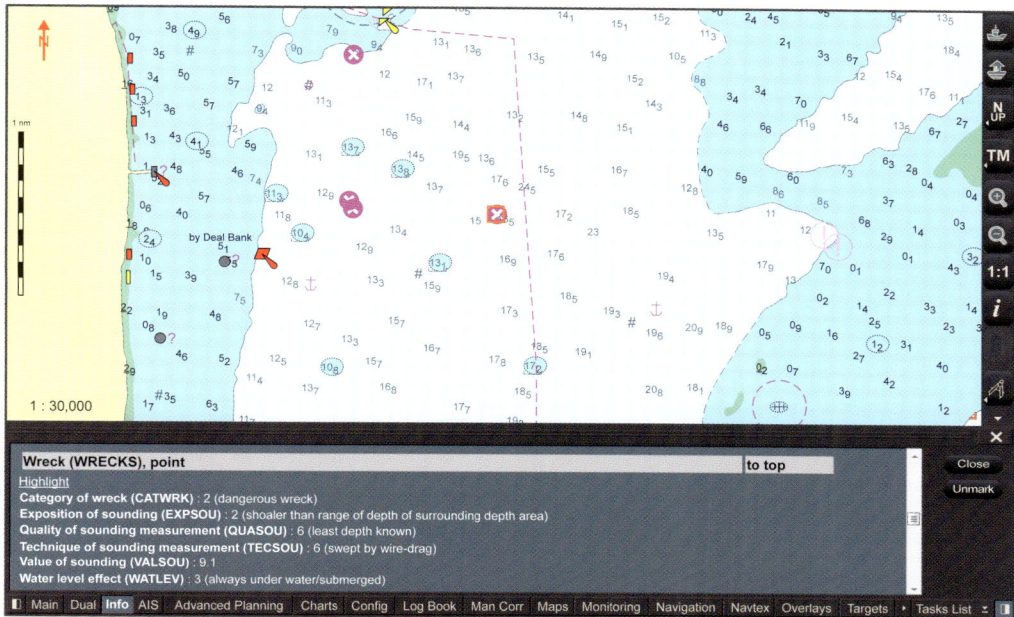

Figure 36: A consequence of the disparity between calculated and available safety contours is that not all isolated dangers are dangers at all. Note the dotted line of the safety contour in the right of the screenshot, symbolising a contour of low accuracy (Transas)

c. Chart Display

The display of charted information can now be configured to suit the needs of the NO. This is achieved by selecting an appropriate IMO display category, such as the *'Standard Display'* (see EW section 2.3.5 Display Category and Annex F ECDIS Viewing Groups). Additional layers can then be added as required from the *'Other Display'* category, and by turning on the display of information controlled by independent mariner selectors (see EW Annex E Independent Mariner Selectors). The following list provides considerations when configuring the display for route planning:

- Chart display

    – chart accuracy (CATZOCs)

    – chart boundaries

    – contour labels

    – date-dependent objects

    – depth contours

    – four colour depth shades

    – full light lines

    – graticule

    – highlight date dependent

    – highlight document

- highlight info

- isolated dangers not a danger to own ship's navigation

- latest corrections

- names in national language

- nature of seabed

- paper chart or simplified symbols

- plain or symbolised boundaries

- scale minimum (SCAMIN)

- shallow pattern

- shallow water dangers

- spot soundings

- submarine cables and pipelines

- text

- tidal information

- unknown object.

Some systems may provide a more detailed ability to configure the chart display, by allowing the NO to select display layers from a list of display category layers (see Figure 38).

ENC symbology needs to be adequately understood, in particular symbology that has no equivalent in paper charts, such as simplified symbology, plain boundaries and new symbology. The meaning of symbols may be found within *ECDIS Chart 1*, installed in ECDIS for use offline during route planning.

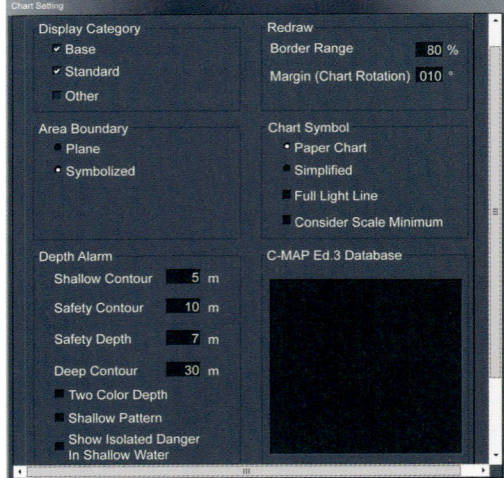
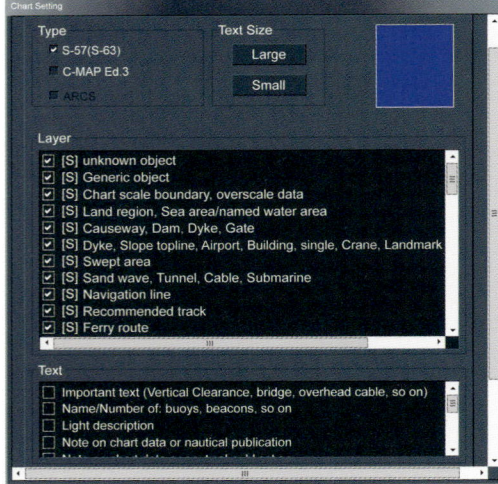

Figures 37 & 38: An example of chart display options that are selectable by the operator (JRC)

It is important to understand exactly what information is displayed when certain selectors or layers are chosen for display, as only then will the NO know whether or not it is relevant to them. It may be that different information is required when planning different parts of the route, such as pilotage waters, coastal areas and open ocean, for example, in which case the display will need to be configured throughout the process. For example, the display of submarine cables and pipelines may only be relevant when planning an anchorage, whereas the choice of two colour shades as opposed to four may be limited to areas of pilotage. The display of four colour depth shading can be seen in Figures 39 and 40.

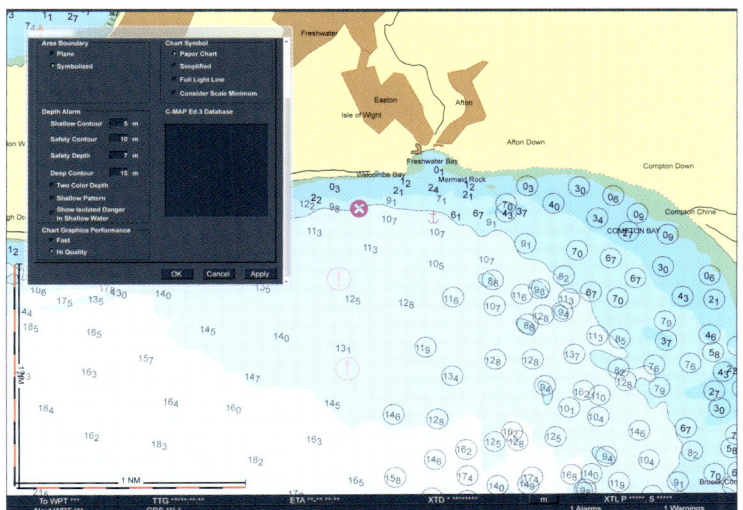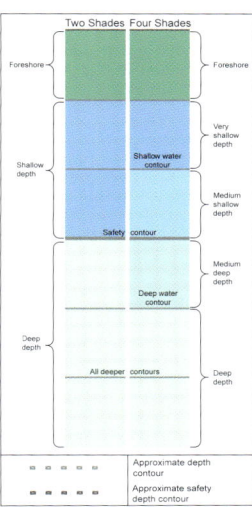

Figures 39 & 40: The option for four colour shading is not mandated but is normally provided (JRC)

The utility of four colour depth shading will depend on the individual vessel and circumstances, but could be used, for example, to highlight the onset depth for shallow water effect, although doing so is dependent upon the availability of the desired depth contour within the SENC. If using four colour depth shades during the planning phase, then values for the shallow (default 2 m) and deep contours (default 30 m) should be input, noting that these contours will not trigger an alarm during route monitoring. Additionally, the display of auxiliary layers provided by integration with other software or equipment should be considered for display, such as:

● Admiralty Information Overlay (AIO)

● NAVTEX.

The *Admiralty Information Overlay* contains additional information that may affect the passage such as T&P NMs and reported navigational hazards incorporated on paper charts that have not yet been included in ENCs. The nature of the overlay means that areas affecting the planned route can quickly be identified, allowing the NO to plan the route around them, if necessary (see Figure 41). Where NAVTEX is integrated with ECDIS, the NO can benefit from displaying the latest navigation warnings (see Figure 42).

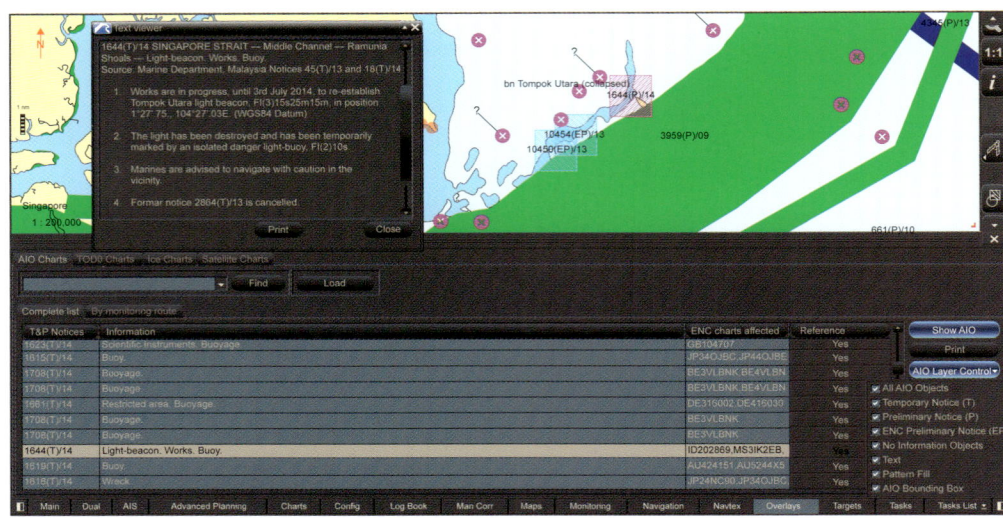

Figure 41: The AIO provides important T&P information that may impact upon a voyage (Transas)

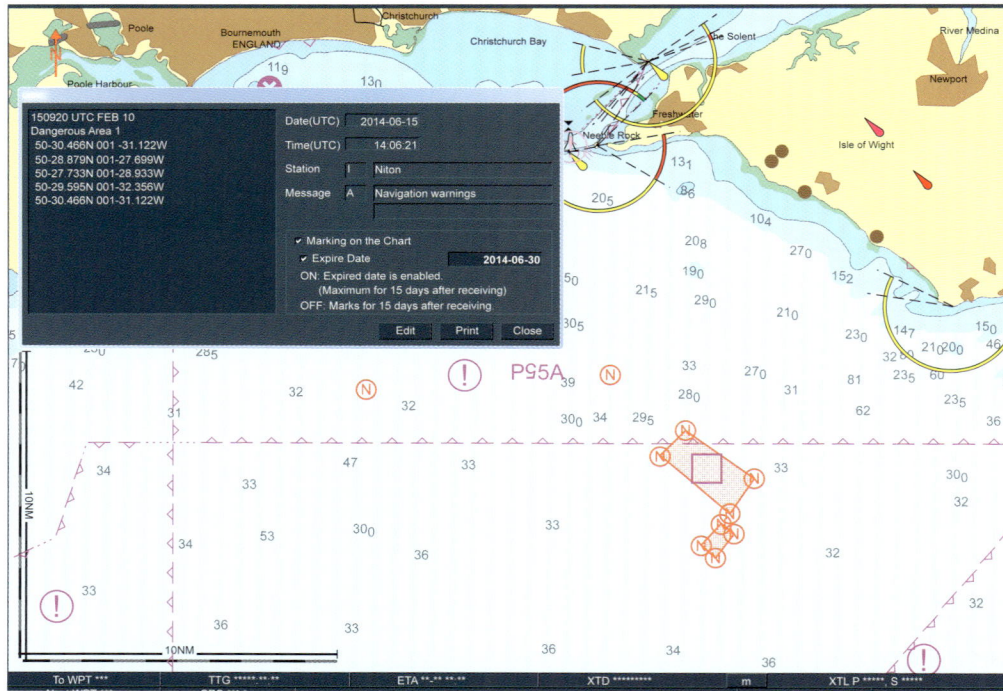

Figure 42: NAVTEX integration with ECDIS allows the display of the latest navigation warnings (JRC)

Configuration of the chart display is a delicate balance between displaying too little information, where important safety information may be hidden, and too much, where information can overlap and be hidden in clutter. The degree of detail depends largely upon the display category chosen. For example, the Base display provides too little information whilst the All Other display category too much. What's important is that careful consideration be given to the relevance of displayed information, with regard to the environment and specifics of the vessel that will be conducting the passage. The documentation of such settings will add consistency to planning, as will the ability to save the customised chart display, which is available on some systems.

> **?** Edition 4.0.0 of the PL mandates the inclusion of a date-dependent object function. This facilitates the display of seasonal objects and provides the planner with visibility of objects such as new Traffic Separation Schemes before they come into force. This is important as route execution may coincide with the in force date.

d. Route Options

The extent of annotation displayed along the route during planning can now be configured. The amount of information available for display will depend on the capabilities and functionality of the ECDIS fitted, such as:

- Route options
  - arrival circles (for use with track control)
  - cross track distance (XTD)
  - distances
  - planned speed
  - true courses
  - turn radius
  - waypoint names
  - wheel over lines.

Certain display options, such as planned speed, may not be available for display until a value is entered by the operator in the route table (see section 3.2.5).

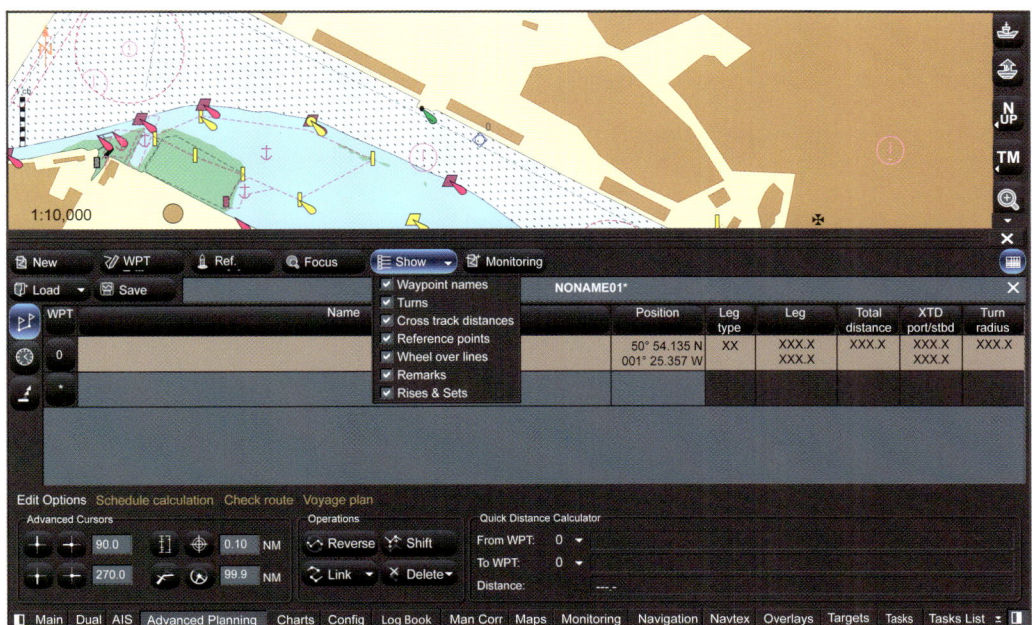

Figure 43: An example of route display options (Transas)

3.2 Route Creation

The detailed physical planning can now commence, covering the entire passage from berth to berth, including those areas where the services of a pilot will be used. The objective is to use all information obtained during the appraisal to create the safest possible route, avoiding actions and activities that could cause damage to the environment whilst taking into account the intended method of execution and monitoring. The IMO Performance Standards for ECDIS state that ECDIS should be able to do the following with regard to route planning:

● It should be possible to carry out route planning including both straight and curved segments

● it should be possible to adjust a planned route alphanumerically and graphically including:

   – adding waypoints to a route

   – deleting waypoints from a route

   – changing the position of a waypoint

● it should be possible to plan one or more alternative routes in addition to the selected route

● the selected route should be clearly distinguishable from the other routes.

 Some ECDIS *Route Planning* functions are more intuitive than others. This can cause frustration. However, with practice and knowledge of the onboard system it will soon get less onerous.

3.2.1   New Route

Open the route planning function and select *'new route'* or equivalent. Some systems will allow the route to be named at this stage. If so, name the route clearly so it can be easily found when it comes to executing the route, for example *'SouthamptonStockholm20May15'* (from, to, date of planned passage). Prior to adding waypoints it is important to understand the difference between the various ENC usage bands (also known as navigational purpose bands), as the scale of chart when planning the route should be appropriate and fit the availability of chart data, as only then will the level of detail be sufficient (see Table 1 and Figures 44-49).

Usage Band or Navigational Purpose Band	Name	Scale Range
1	Overview	<1:1,499,999
2	General	1:350,000 – 1:1,499,999
3	Coastal	1:90,000 – 1:349,999
4	Approach	1:22,000 – 1:89,999
5	Harbour	1:4,000 – 1:21,999
6	Berthing	>1:4,000

Table 1: Definition of usage bands (IHO)

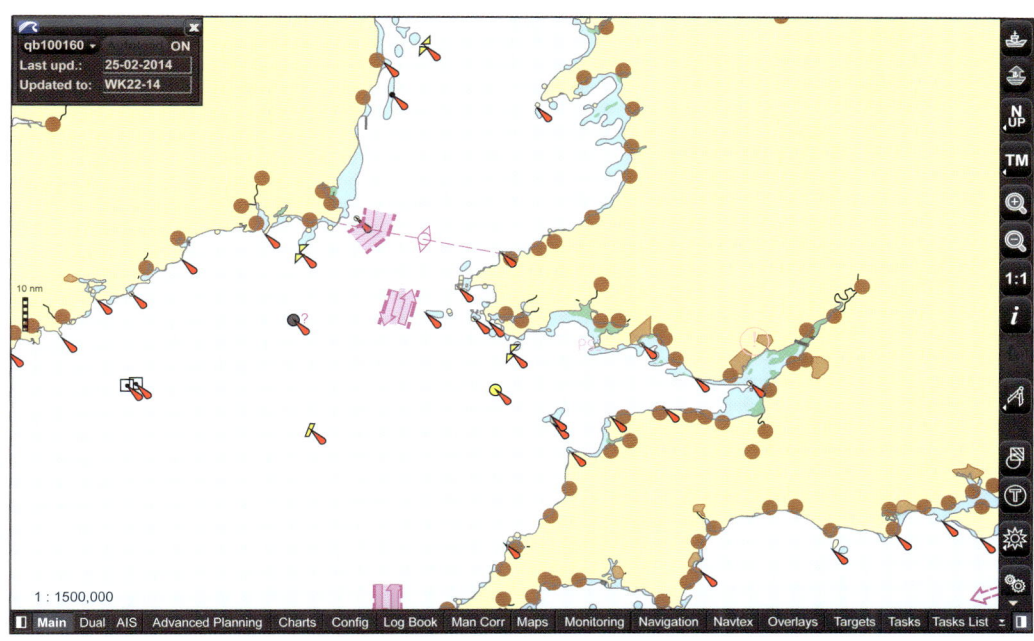

Figure 44: Usage band 1 – Overview. Note that the first number of the chart *gb100160* refers to the usage band (Transas)

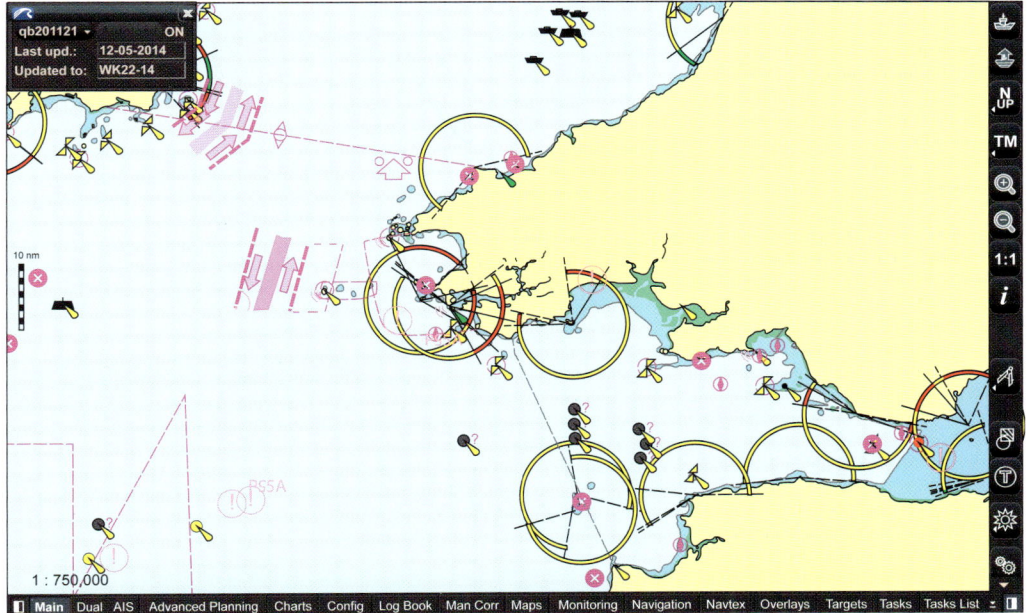

Figure 45: Usage band 2 – General (Transas)

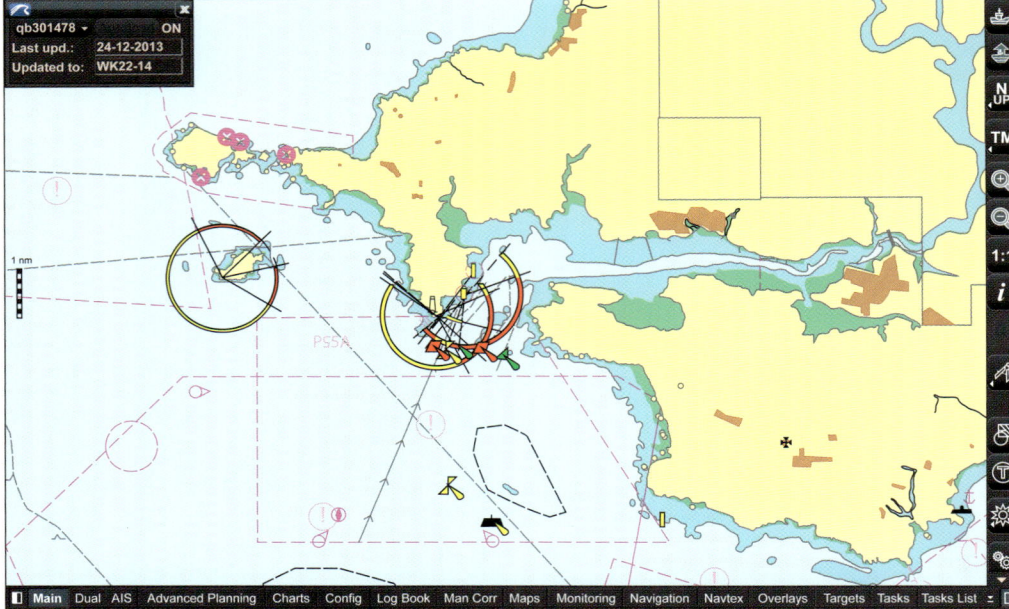

Figure 46: Usage band 3 – Coastal (Transas)

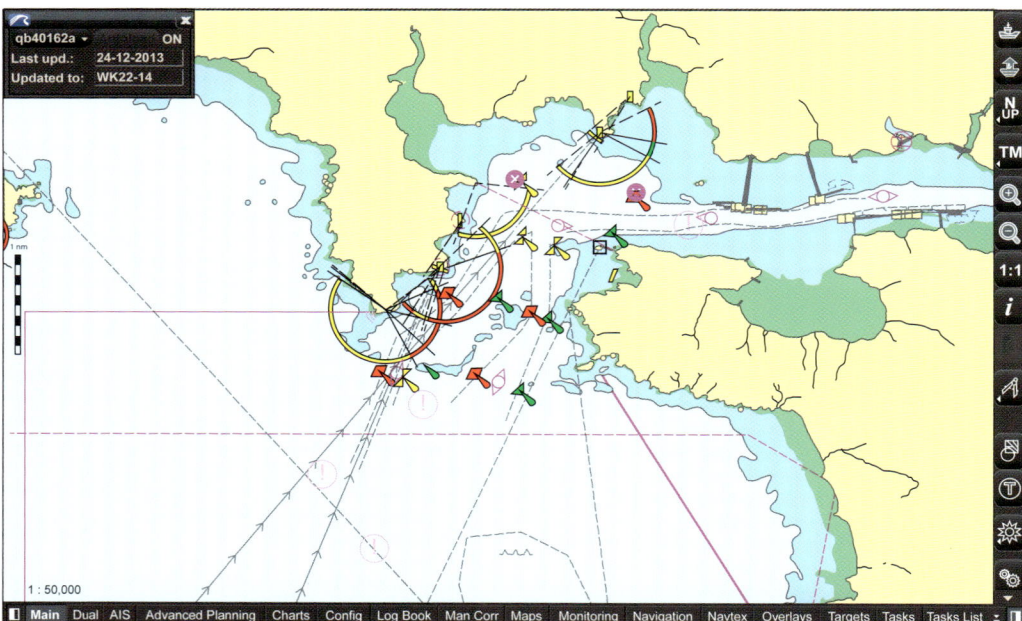

Figure 47: Usage band 4 – Approach (Transas)

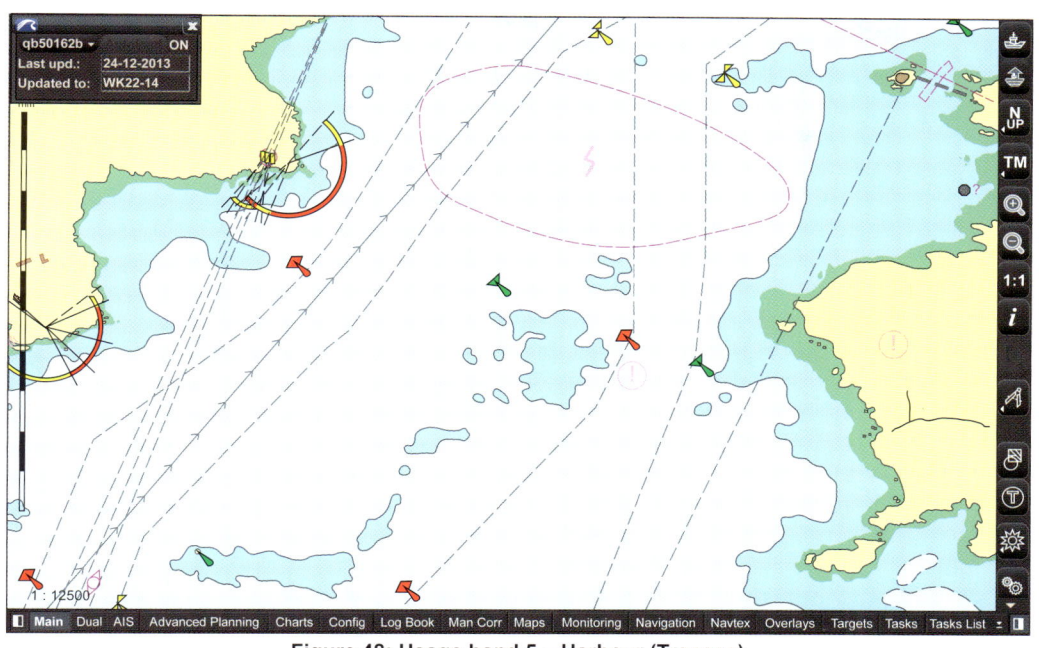

Figure 48: Usage band 5 – Harbour (Transas)

Figure 49: Usage band 6 – Berthing (Transas)

The scale ranges in Table 1 are indicative only. This is because most ENCs are derived from paper charts. This means that ENCs not only have similar characteristics in terms of content and generalisation to the paper chart source, but cell limits and compilation scales are also generally comparable. The scales chosen for ENC usage bands will depend on a variety of factors. For example, coastal ENCs must not only take into account the availability of source data, but the nature of the area and density of shipping, whilst approach, harbour and berthing charts must additionally consider the size of the harbour and the extent of the port area. As these factors vary from port to port, chart coverage and scales within usage bands will vary as a result.

3.2.2   Adding Waypoints

There are a number of ways to construct a route on ECDIS and the best method is very much a case of personal preference whilst taking into account the capabilities of the ECDIS in use. The method employed may depend on the proximity of the destination, although efficient route planning on ECDIS should minimise the requirement for zooming in and out, as this will prolong planning and cause frustration. The method described below involves planning a route on small scale ENCs before positioning waypoints on appropriate large scale ENCs. This is similar to planning on paper charts, where planning charts are used to outline the route prior to commencing detailed planning. This is opposed to planning on large scale ENCs from the outset, where perspective can be easily lost. When deciding what method to use, bear in mind that when a waypoint is positioned in ECDIS it is input as a geographical location and is not assigned to a specific chart, but to all installed charts that cover that location. Therefore, a route displayed on a small scale chart as an overview, can be analysed in greater detail by zooming and loading larger scale charts.

 **Prior to constructing the route it is prudent to locate the start and end locations and check the latitude and longitude. This is necessary as many world ports have the same or similar names. Some ECDIS provide a database of world ports to facilitate this.**

Using small scale ENCs, begin by adding a waypoint in the vicinity of the start location using the cursor. When two waypoints are inserted the system automatically joins them together to form legs, which are rhumb lines by default. Remaining on small scale ENCs, and armed with the knowledge acquired during the appraisal, construct the route by adding successive waypoints, completing the route by adding a waypoint in the vicinity of the destination. The position of waypoints need only be approximate at this stage as they will be fine-tuned in due course. The method described is a graphical method of constructing a route using the cursor to enter waypoints. An alternative method is to use the tabular method, where the latitude and longitude of waypoints are entered manually in the *Route Table*. Leg details such as true course and distance can be viewed in the route table, or chosen for display, where available, along the route itself.

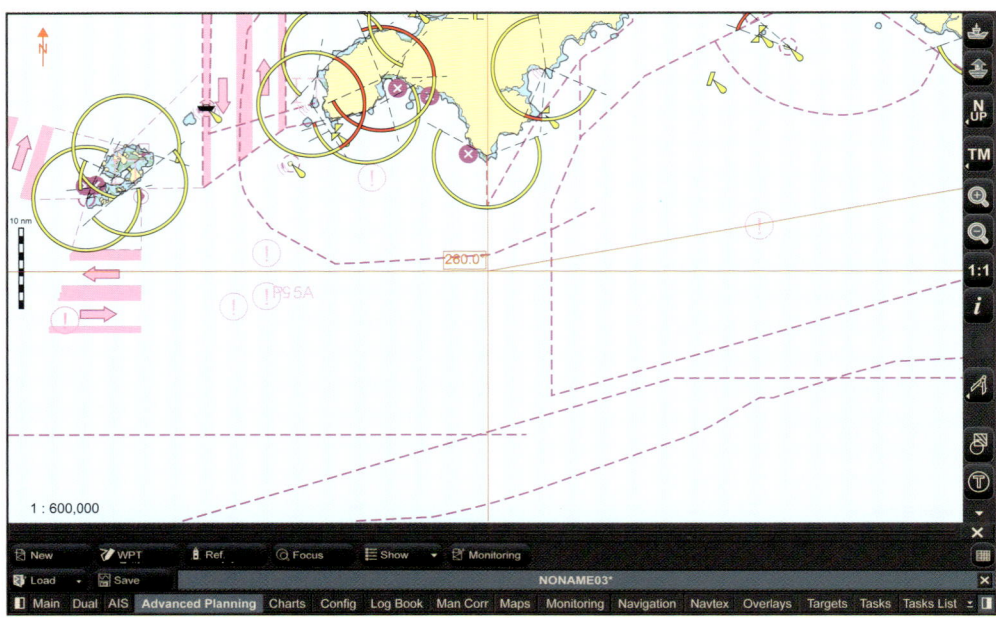

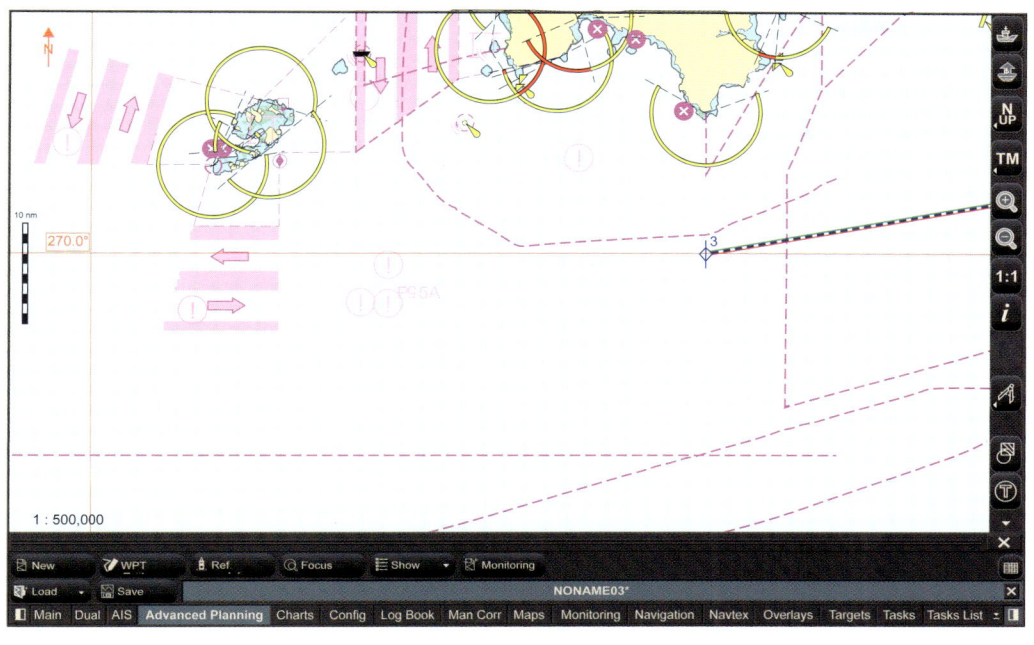

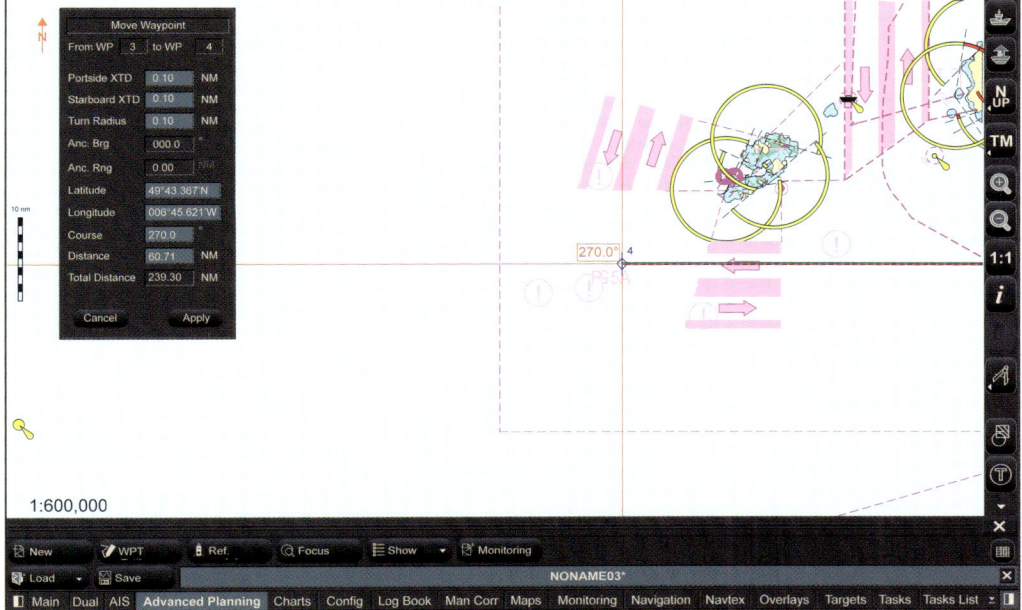

Figures 50-52: Example of the graphical method of waypoint entry using the cursor (Transas)

3.2.3 Adjusting Waypoints

Once an approximation of the entire route has been achieved on small scale charts, it is necessary to return to the start position and conduct more accurate planning by fine-tuning waypoints using appropriate large scale charts.

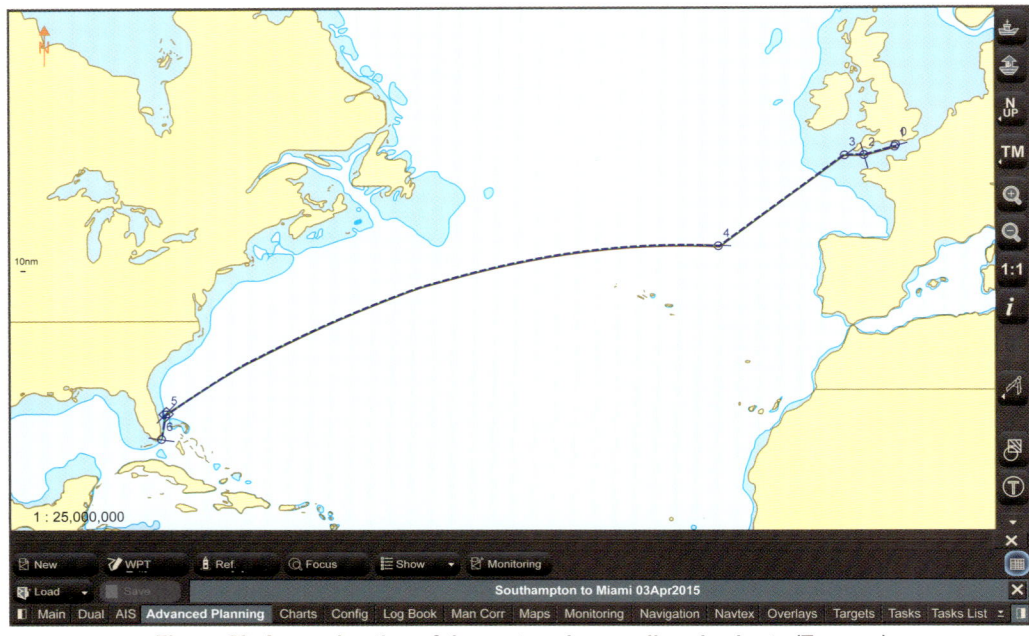

Figure 53: Approximation of the route using small scale charts (Transas)

Waypoints should be placed as accurately as possible, noting that it is normally possible to achieve whole number courses, rather than decimal, by manipulating such data in the route table. This may be required in areas that require hand steering. Some systems are capable of achieving this within the graphical method, as in Figure 52. The following are considerations when adjusting waypoints:

- With particular regard to the vessel:
  - draught in relation to the available depth of water and minimum UKC
  - effect on vessel draught and turning circle during course alteration
    - o planned speed
    - o effect of expected tidal stream
    - o effect of expected current
    - o increase in draught due to squat and heel effect
  - manoeuvring characteristics
  - positions where a change in machinery status is required
  - positions where additional bridge or engine room manning is required
- with particular regard to the route:
  - adequate cross track distance (XTD)
  - alterations of speed en-route
  - avoidance of danger areas
  - considerations relating to the protection of the marine environment
  - contingency planning
    - o deep water

- o   port of refuge or safe anchorage in the event of an emergency
- o   shore-based emergency response arrangements and equipment
- o   nature of the cargo and of the emergency itself
- depth of water
- limitations of night passage
- location of course alterations
- method and frequency of position fixing
  - o   primary and secondary fixing options
  - o   indication of areas where accuracy of position fixing is critical
  - o   indication of areas where maximum reliability of position fixing must be obtained
  - o   availability of visual and radar fixing to cross check accuracy of GNSS
  - o   radar image overlay
  - o   parallel indices
  - o   astronomical observation
- safe speed and proximity of navigational hazards
- safety and efficiency of navigation
- tidal restrictions
- use of ships' routeing, reporting systems and vessel traffic services.

The relevance of the considerations above will depend upon the nature of the environment through which the route is being planned. Certain areas may take more planning and skill than others and require different techniques and tools. For example, pilotage planning will require a different set of tools to planning in open ocean. The manufacturer may provide tools to facilitate planning in this regard, such as:

- Pilotage
  - advance and transfer
  - anchorage planning
  - blind pilotage planning
  - clearing line (mandatory)
  - distance to wheel over marks
  - headmark, sternmark and beammark tools
  - tidal stream adjustment for wheel over
  - wheel over bearings
- coastal
  - nominal range of lights
  - parallel indices
- open ocean
  - great circle lines (mandatory).

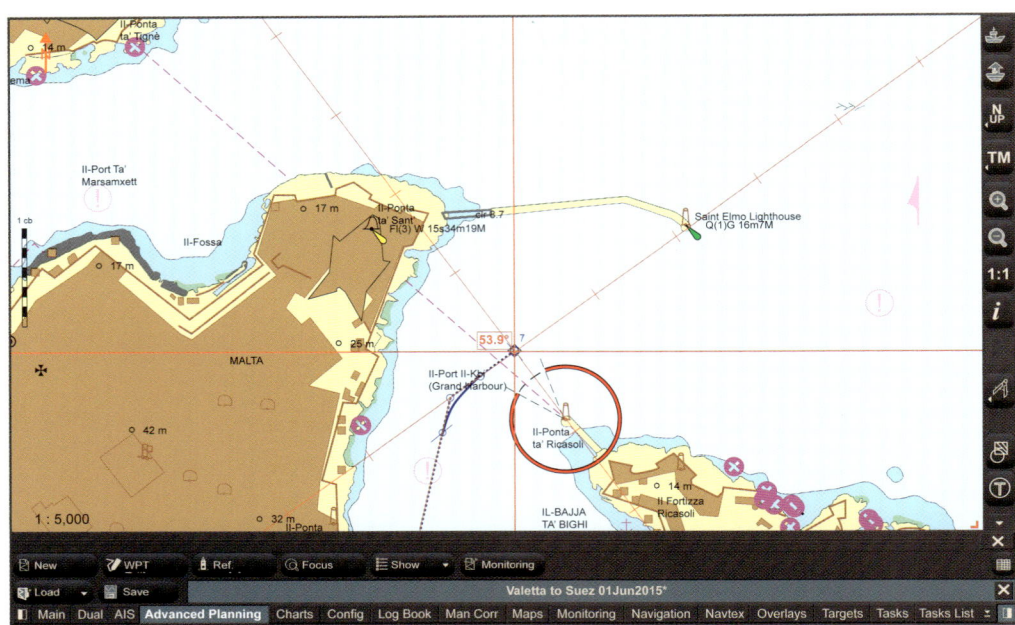

Figure 54: Example of pilotage planning using a headmark and beammark tool (Transas)

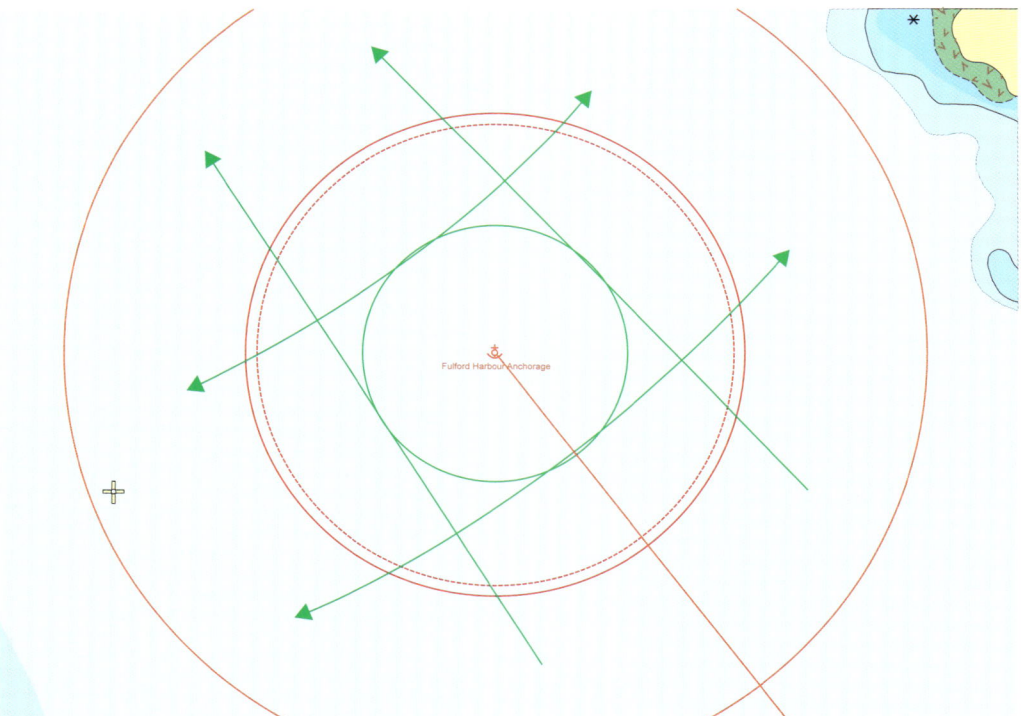

Figure 55: Example of detailed anchorage planning (OSI)

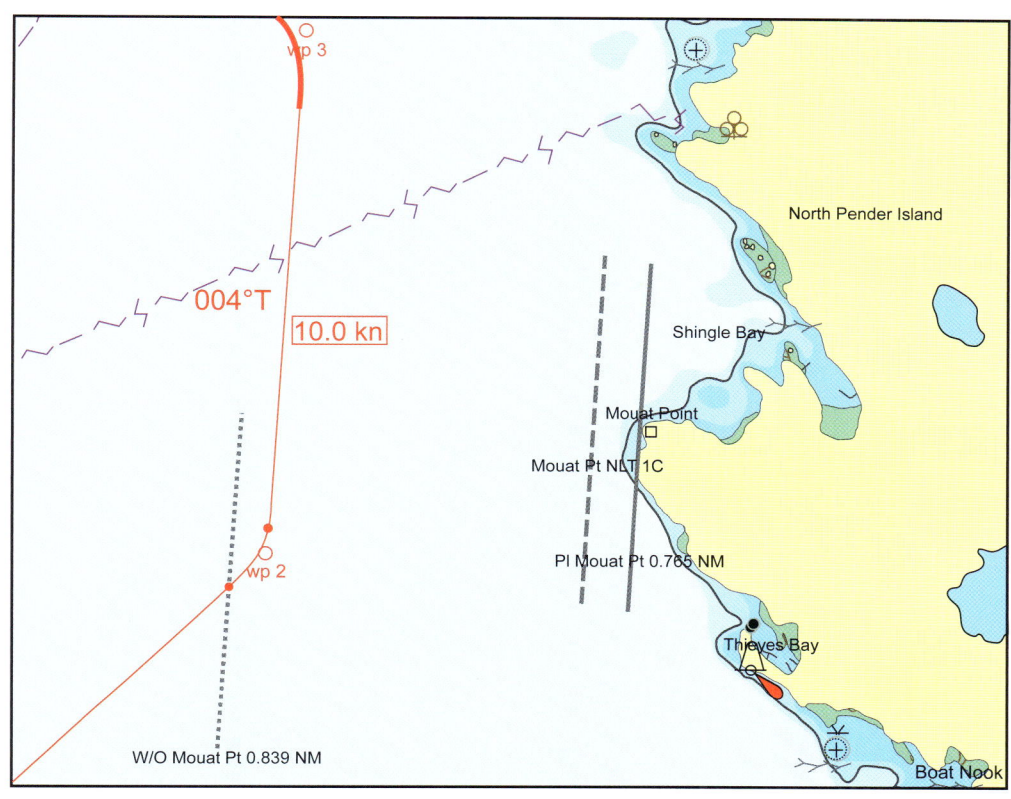

Figure 56: Example of blind pilotage planning (OSI)

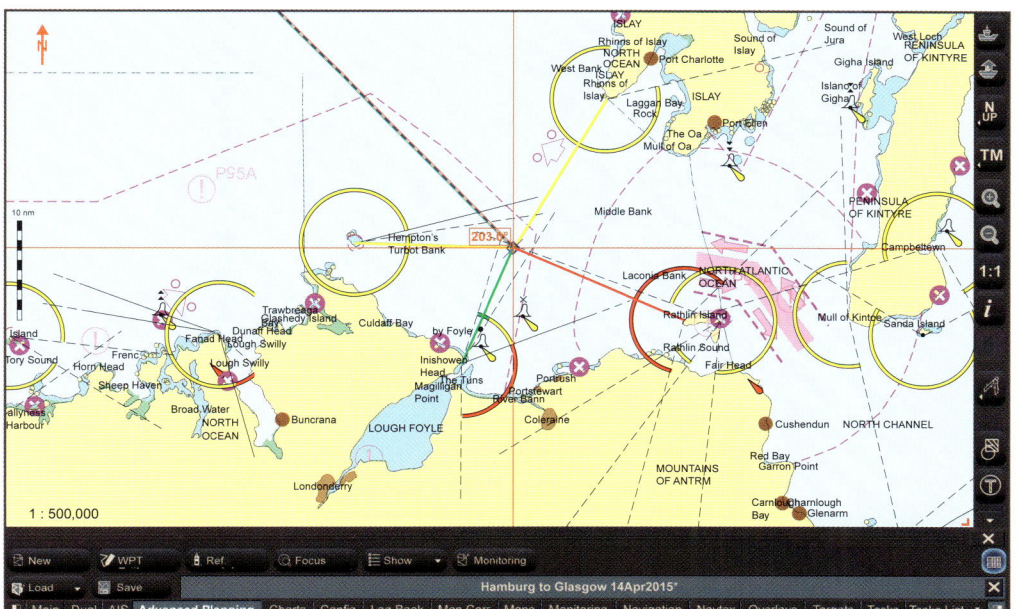

Figure 57: Example of route planning taking into account the nominal range of lights (Transas)

By default, ECDIS will create legs as rhumb lines, but this can be changed to a great circle line for ocean passages by adjusting leg properties. When doing so, great circle lines can usually be divided into a series of individual rhumb lines for ease of navigation, either by longitude or a set distance. Some ECDIS manufacturers also provide the ability to restrict the latitude of a great circle line by entering a *'limiting latitude'*. If required, a combination of rhumb lines and great circles can be used to form a composite track.

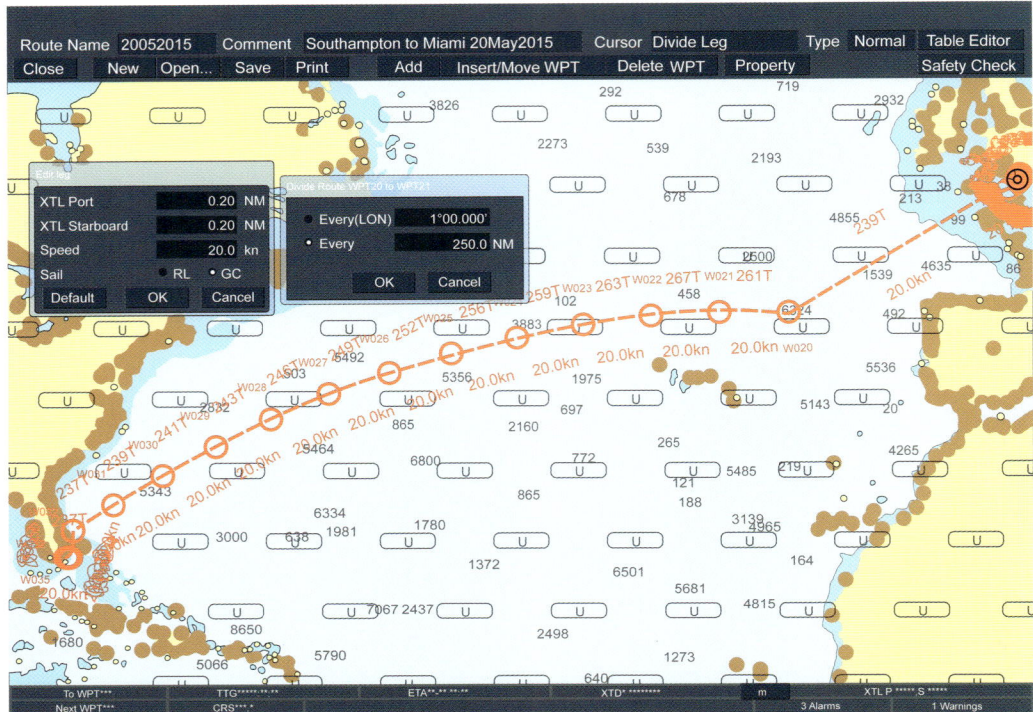

Figure 58: Rhumb lines and great circle lines can be used to form a composite track. Here, a great circle line is divided into a series of rhumb lines for ease of navigation (JRC)

> **i**   A small number of ECDIS are capable of displaying charts with Gnomonic and Polar Stereographic projections for navigation at high latitudes.

Checks should be conducted for quality control throughout route planning, using the following sources of information:

- Visual check of ENC
    - ENC accuracy and CATZOCs
    - gaps in ENC coverage
    - isolated dangers outside of the safety contour
    - where possible, comparison of equivalent RNC
- cursor pick
    - unknown object symbol [SY(QUESMRK1)]
    - objects and areas where more information is required

- digital publications
  - list of lights
  - list of radio signals
- AIO layer
  - T&P NM information.

The cursor pick function can be used to access useful additional information contained within the SENC. This may include diagrams, images and text documents to assist the planner (see Figures 59-63).

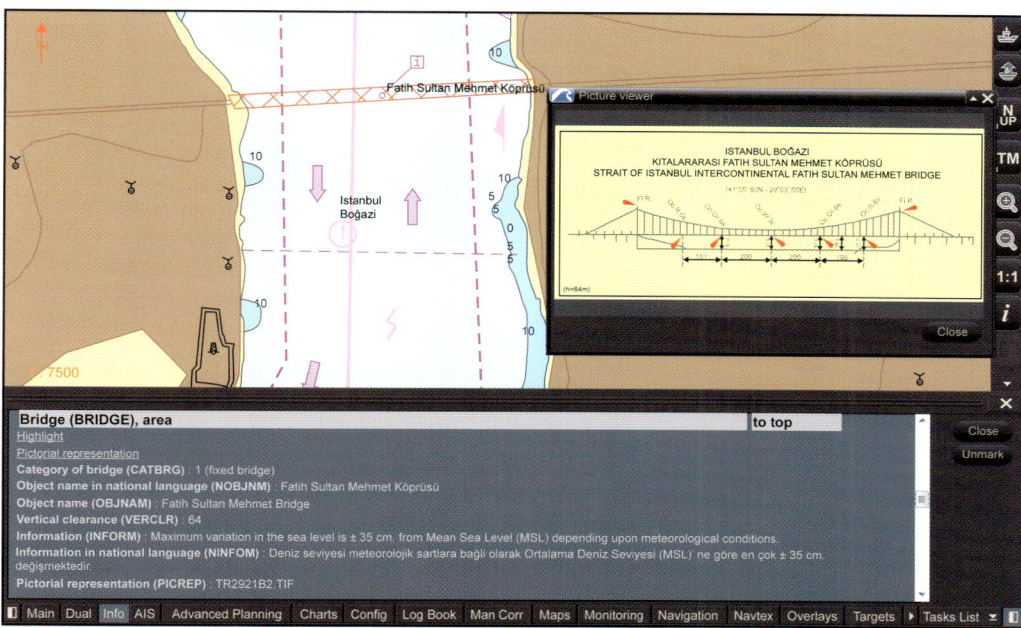

Figure 59: Pick reports can contain useful information displayed graphically, such as clearance information... (Transas)

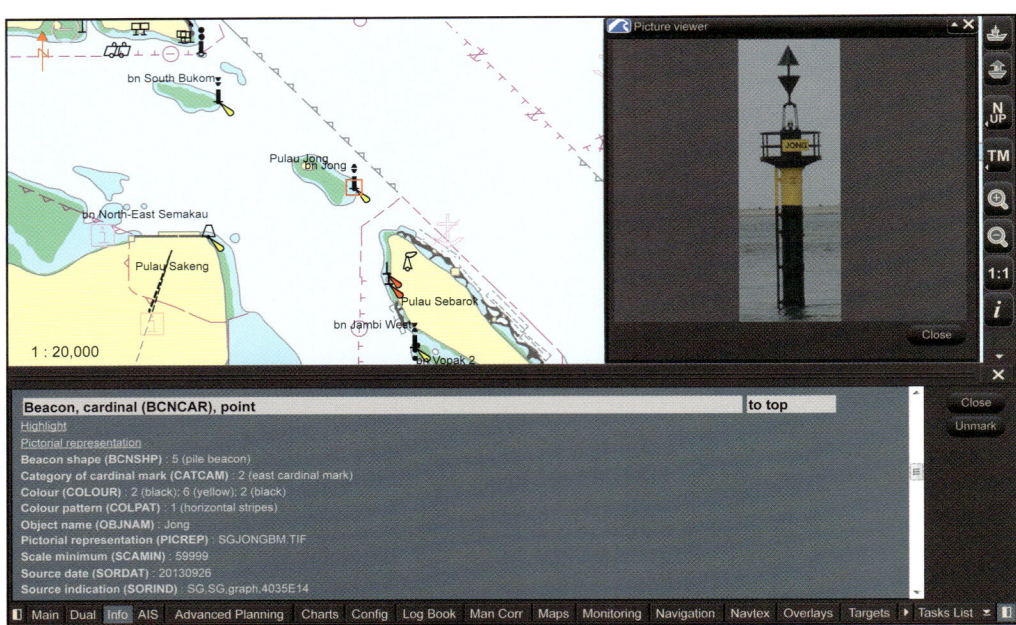

Figure 60: ...images of beacons... (Transas)

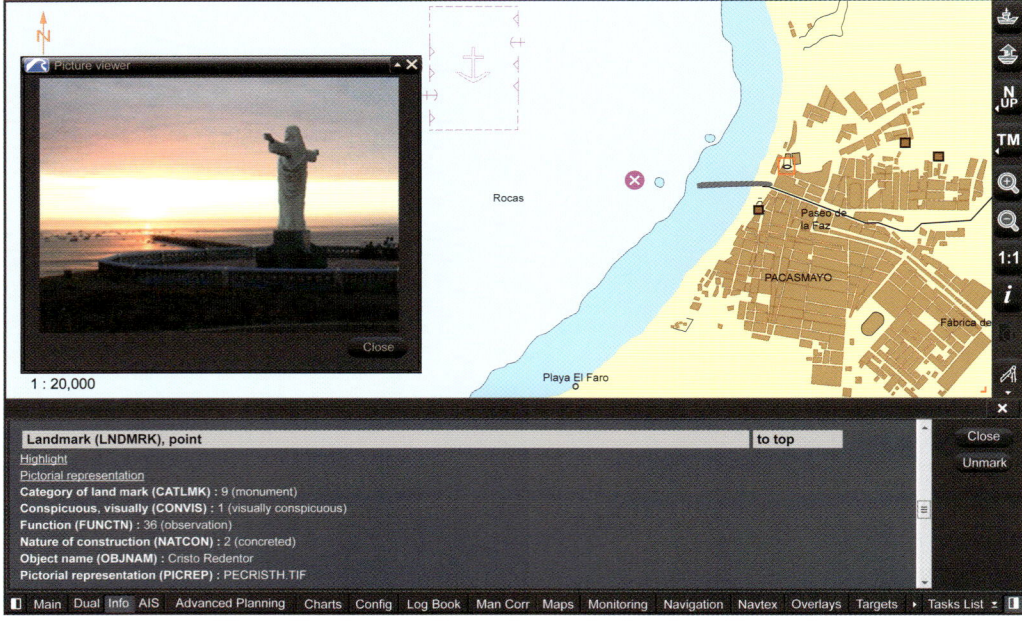

Figure 61: ...images of conspicuous landmarks... (Transas)

Figure 62: …to images of ports and harbours… (Transas)

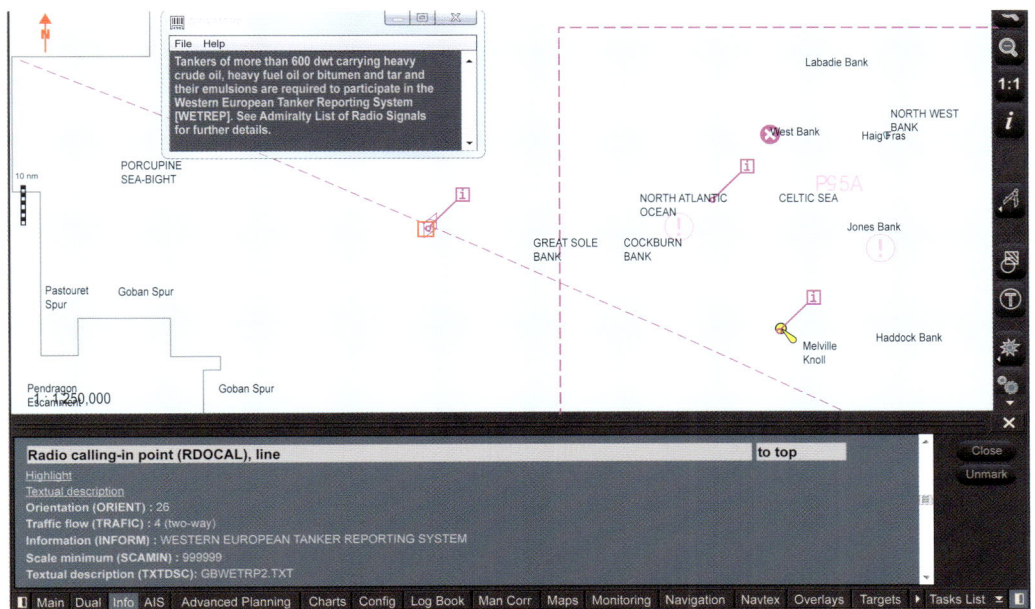

Figure 63: …and textual information (Transas)

 The exchange language of ENCs is English and so access to information written and presented in national languages will depend upon the chart producer providing it. Additional text in national language may or may not be available.

Additionally, digital publications are of use when details of radio signals and light signal information are not contained within the SENC.

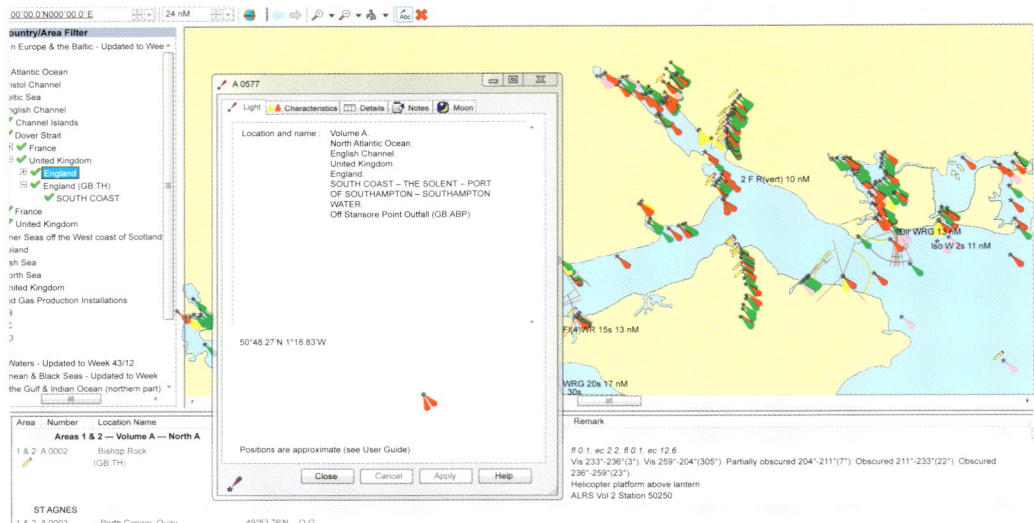

Figure 64: Admiralty digital list of lights (UKHO)

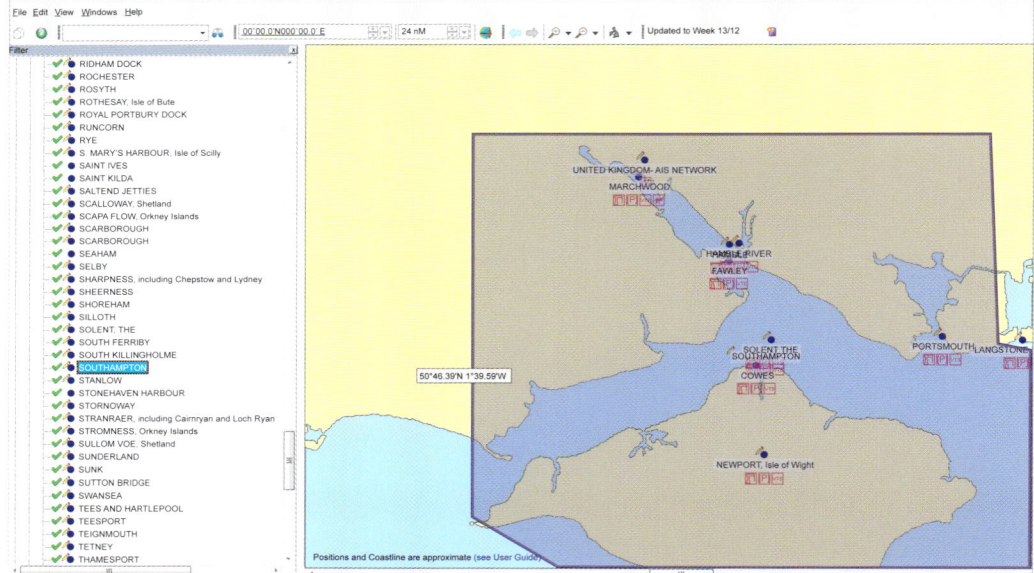

Figure 65: Admiralty digital list of radio signals (UKHO)

3.2.4 Multiple Routes

When calculating the safety contour during the appraisal, there will be times when the value at the destination differs from that calculated for the departure. This may be due to different tidal conditions or a change in draught, for example. In such cases, it may be desirable to construct multiple routes instead of a single berth to berth plan. This would allow various stages of the route to be planned using different safety contour values, optimising the availability of safe water. When doing so, the linking waypoints should be checked to ensure that they are consistent with the end of the previous route and the start of the next one. Additionally, clear annotation is required to inform the operator of the need to load a new route for monitoring and to change the value of the safety contour.

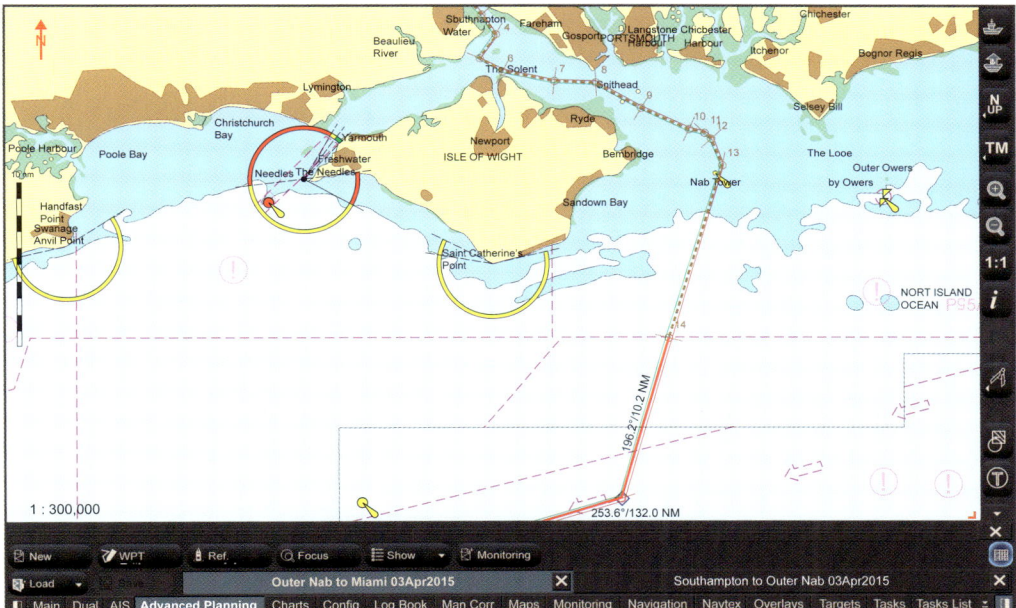

Figures 66 & 67: Some systems embed safety depth and safety contour information within a planned route. This allows the operator to be prompted to change these values when a new route is loaded, if they differ from those set for the current route (Transas)

3.2.5 Route Table

Once the detailed planning has been completed, elements of the route can be fine-tuned or changed by completing the route table. Doing so will provide essential detail with which speed, time and distance calculations can be made. For example, ECDIS cannot calculate the ETA without the provision of a planned speed, or the overall speed required without an ETD and ETA. These calculated values will be used by the operator to manage speed and ETAs, both at waypoints and the final destination, during the monitoring phase. Values for the following can normally be manually entered for individual legs:

- Arrival radius (for use with track control)
- course
- distance
- ETA
- ETD
- leg property (RL or GC)
- planned speed
- rate of turn
- remarks
- time zone
- turn radius
- waypoint name
- waypoint latitude and longitude
- XTD (port and starboard).

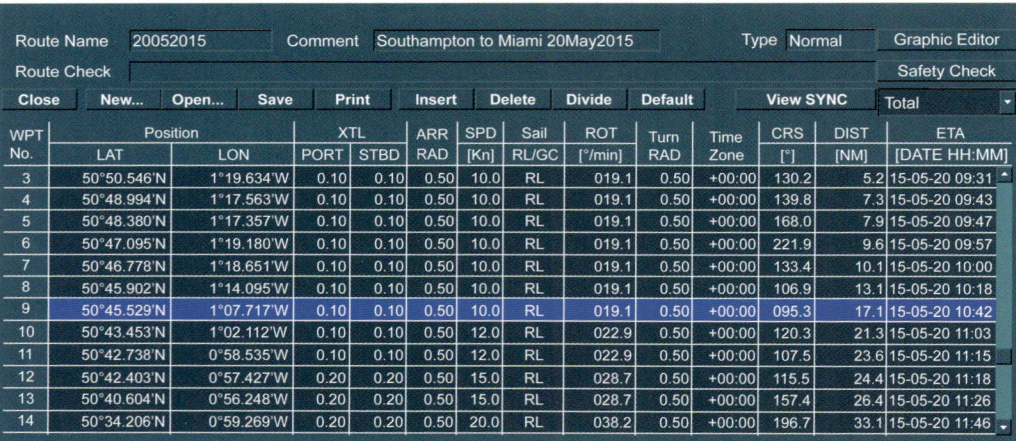

WPT No.	Position		XTL		ARR RAD	SPD [Kn]	Sail RL/GC	ROT [°/min]	Turn RAD	Time Zone	CRS [°]	DIST [NM]	ETA [DATE HH:MM]
	LAT	LON	PORT	STBD									
3	50°50.546'N	1°19.634'W	0.10	0.10	0.50	10.0	RL	019.1	0.50	+00:00	130.2	5.2	15-05-20 09:31
4	50°48.994'N	1°17.563'W	0.10	0.10	0.50	10.0	RL	019.1	0.50	+00:00	139.8	7.3	15-05-20 09:43
5	50°48.380'N	1°17.357'W	0.10	0.10	0.50	10.0	RL	019.1	0.50	+00:00	168.0	7.9	15-05-20 09:47
6	50°47.095'N	1°19.180'W	0.10	0.10	0.50	10.0	RL	019.1	0.50	+00:00	221.9	9.6	15-05-20 09:57
7	50°46.778'N	1°18.651'W	0.10	0.10	0.50	10.0	RL	019.1	0.50	+00:00	133.4	10.1	15-05-20 10:00
8	50°45.902'N	1°14.095'W	0.10	0.10	0.50	10.0	RL	019.1	0.50	+00:00	106.9	13.1	15-05-20 10:18
9	50°45.529'N	1°07.717'W	0.10	0.10	0.50	10.0	RL	019.1	0.50	+00:00	095.3	17.1	15-05-20 10:42
10	50°43.453'N	1°02.112'W	0.10	0.10	0.50	12.0	RL	022.9	0.50	+00:00	120.3	21.3	15-05-20 11:03
11	50°42.738'N	0°58.535'W	0.10	0.10	0.50	12.0	RL	022.9	0.50	+00:00	107.5	23.6	15-05-20 11:15
12	50°42.403'N	0°57.427'W	0.20	0.20	0.50	15.0	RL	028.7	0.50	+00:00	115.5	24.4	15-05-20 11:18
13	50°40.604'N	0°56.248'W	0.20	0.20	0.50	15.0	RL	028.7	0.50	+00:00	157.4	26.4	15-05-20 11:26
14	50°34.206'N	0°59.269'W	0.20	0.20	0.50	20.0	RL	038.2	0.50	+00:00	196.7	33.1	15-05-20 11:46

Figure 68: The route table offers an alternative to plotting waypoints graphically and allows route elements such as course, speed and distance to be adjusted manually (JRC)

Once the route table is complete, elements of the planned route such as speed, time, distance and likely fuel consumption can be checked against those calculations made during the appraisal. At this point, any significant differences can be highlighted and the plan changed accordingly, if required. For example, it may be necessary to refine the ETD, ETA or overall planned speed. Of particular importance is the value entered for XTD, as it is this value that defines the boundaries for the route check. This must be carefully considered to provide adequate sea room in case of lateral separation from the route, deviations for collision avoidance and nature of the environment.

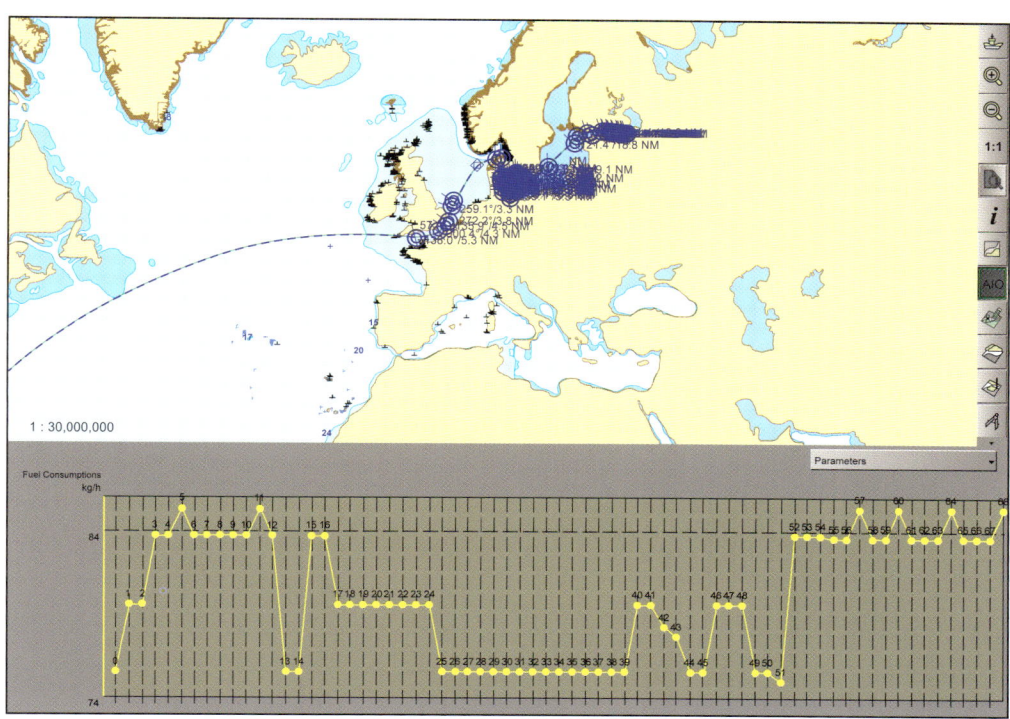

Figure 69: Example of ECDIS passage planning software being used to predict fuel consumption during a planned passage (Transas)

When satisfied with the plan and its associated elements, name the route and save it, if this has not already been done. If ECDIS is connected to a printer then details of the planned route can now be printed (see Figure 70).

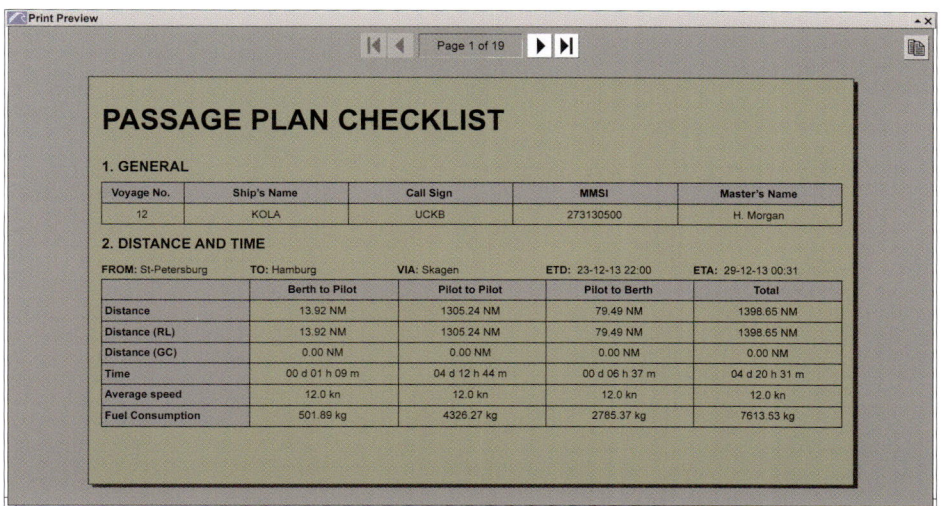

Figure 70: Details of the planned route can be printed (Transas)

> **i** Facilities and availability for receiving accurate weather routeing and forecasting should be sought for the duration of the passage.

3.3 Supplementary Information

The ability to insert information via *'danger highlight'*, notes and features using mariner's navigational objects (see EW 3.7 Mariner's Navigational Objects), allows the NO to annotate the planned route for the purpose of alerting, informing and reminding the operator of potential dangers and actions to be taken at various points during the passage. The quantity of additional information should be limited to that which is necessary to safely and efficiently execute the route, although this will depend upon the complexity of the plan, the nature of the environment and proximity of dangers. The following list provides examples of additional information that could be provided or highlighted:

- Areas of danger
- areas of limited data
- areas of low accuracy data
- areas of no known datum
- areas of overlapping chart data
- areas of poor GNSS coverage
- areas of RCDS mode
- areas of special interest or concern such as anti-piracy measures to be taken
- areas where accuracy of position fixing is critical
- areas where marine environmental protection considerations apply
- areas where maximum reliability of position fixing must be obtained
- changes in IALA systems of maritime buoyage
- gaps in data
- headmarks, points of interest, fixing points
- international regulations, codes and guidelines
- no go lines
- planned changes in speed
- planned changes of safety depth and safety contour values
- planned time zone changes
- points of 'no return' and contingency decisions
- ships' routeing and reporting systems with instructions
- small land areas that may be difficult to see particularly when covered with text
- sunrise and sunset times and bearings
- tide and current
- vessel traffic services (VTS)
- weather concerns and measures to be taken
- where multiple routes are used, planned loading of routes.

When adding information to the chart it should be carefully checked to ensure that it does not cover important charted information and that it is prominent in the night palette.

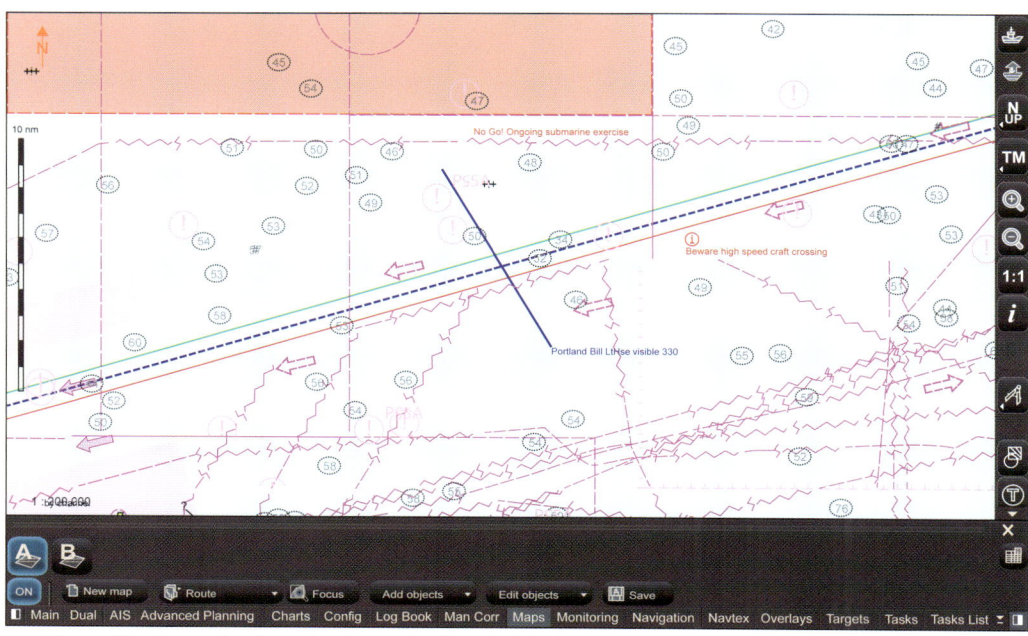

Figure 71: Example of mariner's navigational objects being used to highlight dangers and add navigational and cautionary information (Transas)

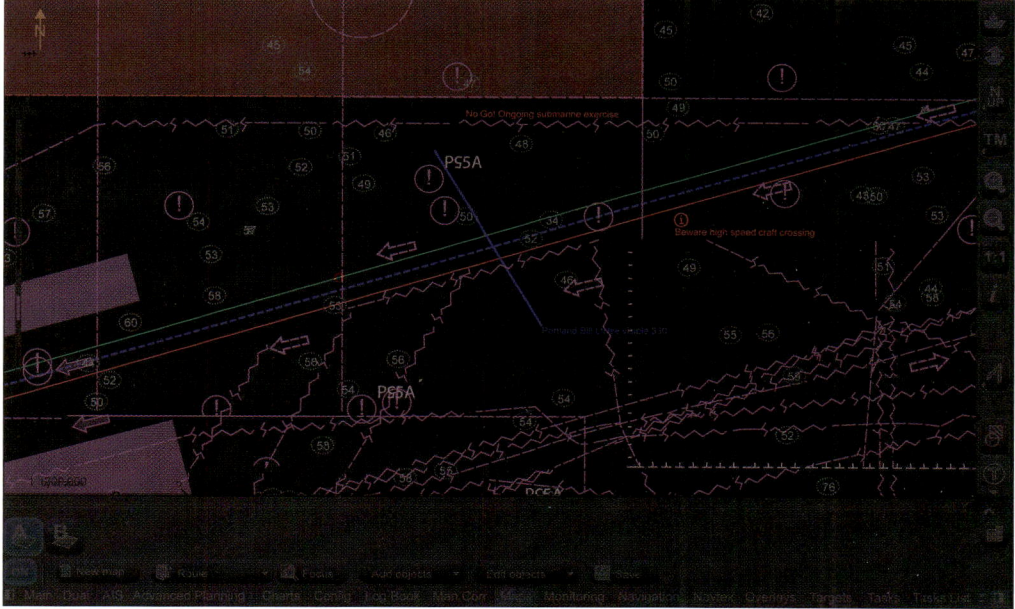

Figure 72: It is always worthwhile checking that mariner's navigational objects are prominent in the night palette, particularly if that area will be transited at night (Transas)

A key feature of mariner's navigational objects is the ability to add a danger highlight. Points and areas inserted using this feature will trigger an alarm during route monitoring when they interact with the *'detection area'* (see EW 2.2.4 Detection Area). This is a useful tool for manually constructing alarmable no-go areas on RNCs, or on ENCs where specific contours do not exist in the SENC (see EP 2.1.9 Safety Contour).

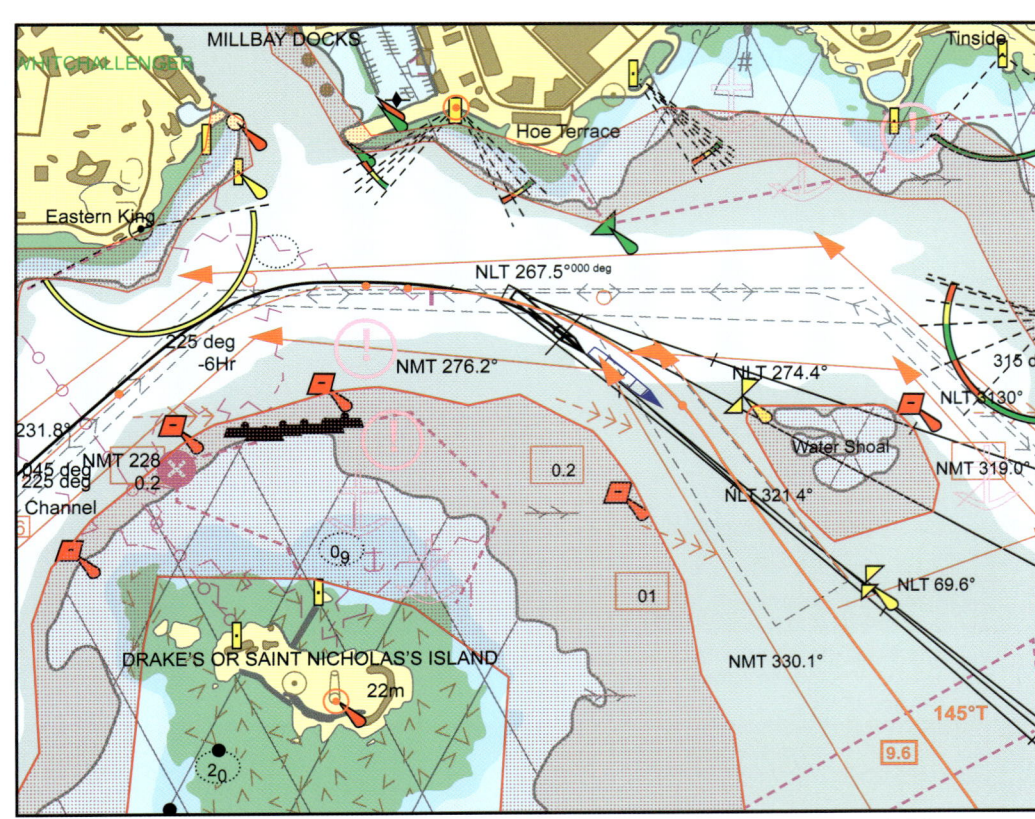

Figure 73: Example of danger highlight being used to indicate no-go areas (OSI)

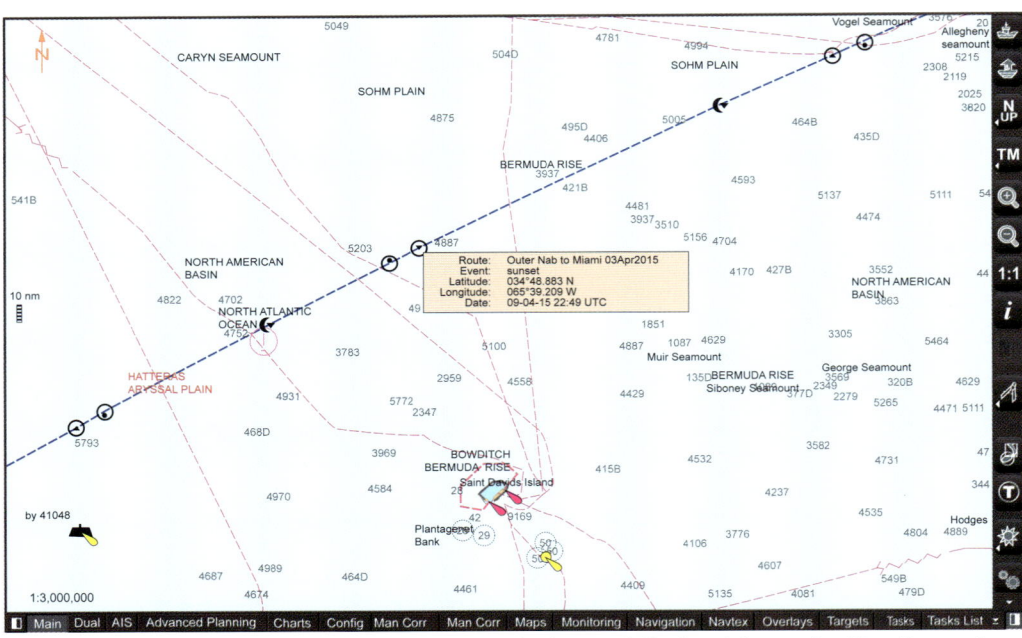

Figure 74: Example of ECDIS being used to calculate and display rising and setting times of astronomical bodies based upon estimates of ship position (Transas)

When complete, all supplementary information files should be named appropriately to ensure the correct files are loaded during the execution phase, and saved.

 Ensure that manual constructs are positioned where they can be clearly seen by the OOW. Where a SCAMIN value is required to be attributed to an inserted mariner's navigational object, ensure it is visible at appropriate scales to avoid it being hidden when the route is executed.

The display of mariner's navigational objects is independent of ECDIS display categories (Base, Standard and All Other). Therefore, the method by which these objects are selected for display will depend upon the specifics of the ECDIS software in use.

3.4 Manual Updates

Where the SENC requires updating manually, the *'manual update'* function can be used to insert symbols, lines and areas. This may be required where information relevant to the planned route is received in the form of a navigational warning, for example, and the sailing date precedes the inclusion of such information within an automatic update. In order to replicate ENC symbology, the operator should have access to any of the chart symbols contained within the PL. Additionally, ECDIS should be capable of sensing indications and alarms related to any manual updates inserted in the SENC, as it does for automatic ENC updates.

Figure 75: Deleted manual update (JRC)　　　Figure 76: Inserted manual update (JRC)

 A deleted feature must appear on the display only when its IMO category and viewing group are selected for display.

 Manual updates of ENC information must be displayed using the same symbology as that contained within the ENC. The additional annotation shown in Figures 75 and 76 distinguishes manual updates from ENC information.

3.5 Route Check

The created route must now be checked for potential dangers in case any have been overlooked during route creation. ECDIS will conduct a check for charted dangers, unsafe depths and potential hazards, but importantly this check is conducted <u>only</u> within the confines of the specified XTD. The route check will detect the following danger to navigation parameters within the user-specified XTD, generating an indication when it does so:

- If a route is planned across the safety contour

- if a route is planned closer than a user-specified distance from the boundary of a prohibited area or a geographic area for which special conditions exist, such as:

  - anchorage area

  - areas to be avoided

  - caution area

  - inshore traffic zone

  - marine farm/aquaculture

  - military practice area

  - offshore production area

  - PSSA (Particularly Sensitive Sea Area)

  - restricted area

  - seaplane landing area

  - submarine transit lane

  - traffic separation zone

  - user-defined areas to be avoided

- if a route is planned closer than a user-specified distance from a point object, such as:

  - a fixed or floating aid to navigation

  - isolated danger.

The 'user-specified distance' stated above refers to the width of the XTD. The capabilities of ECDIS with regard to the route check vary considerably and some ECDIS may have additional functionality within the route check, such as:

- Configuration of route check criteria:

  - prohibited areas

  - areas or a geographic area for which special conditions exist

- detection of soundings equal to or less than the safety depth value

- detection of additional layers, such as:

  - anti-piracy

  - NAVTEX

- draught and UKC checked against charted depths within the XTD

- turning data to ensure that planned turns are achievable

- abnormalities in route construction (eg two waypoints in a single location).

3.5.1   Configuration

To optimise the route check it is necessary that all elements are appropriately configured, where possible. It should be remembered that the effectiveness of the system's automatic route check relies on the accuracy of the safety parameters set by the NO. The following are considerations when configuring the route check:

- XTD
- route check parameters
- chart display
- chart scale.

Of critical importance are the values for the XTD. If these values are too small, then dangers within close proximity to the route will not be detected, too large and a huge number of indications will be generated (see Figure 77). Where it is possible to select what areas will be detected in the check, such parameters must be configured carefully to ensure that relevant dangers are detected. It is recommended that such settings are documented within ECDIS procedures to ensure consistency (see Figure 78).

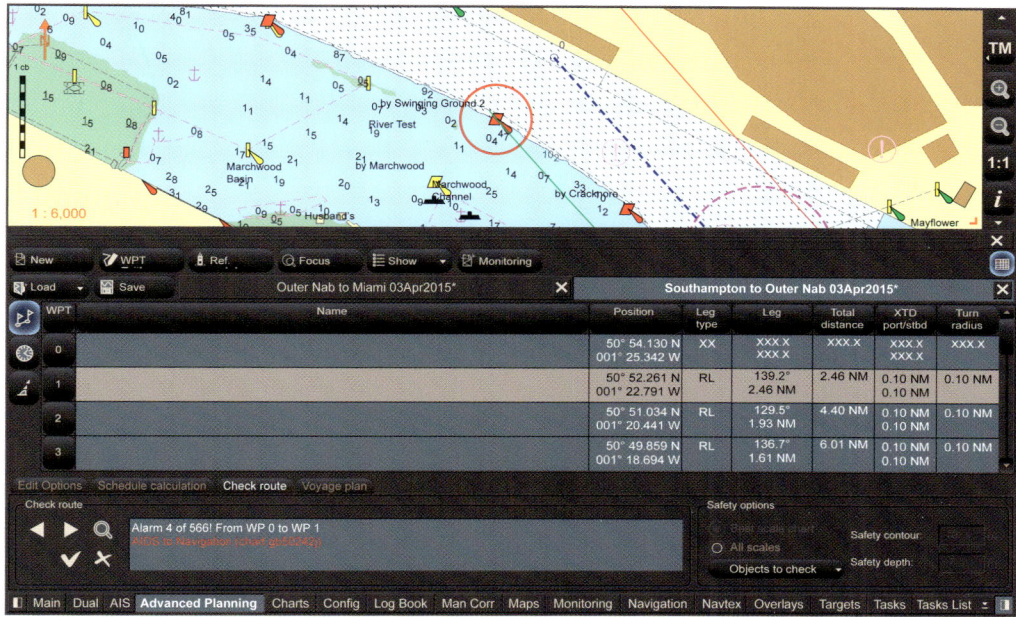

Figure 77: An inappropriately configured XTD can result in hundreds of alarms being generated. Here, the culprit is a XTD that overlaps land and the safety contour (Transas)

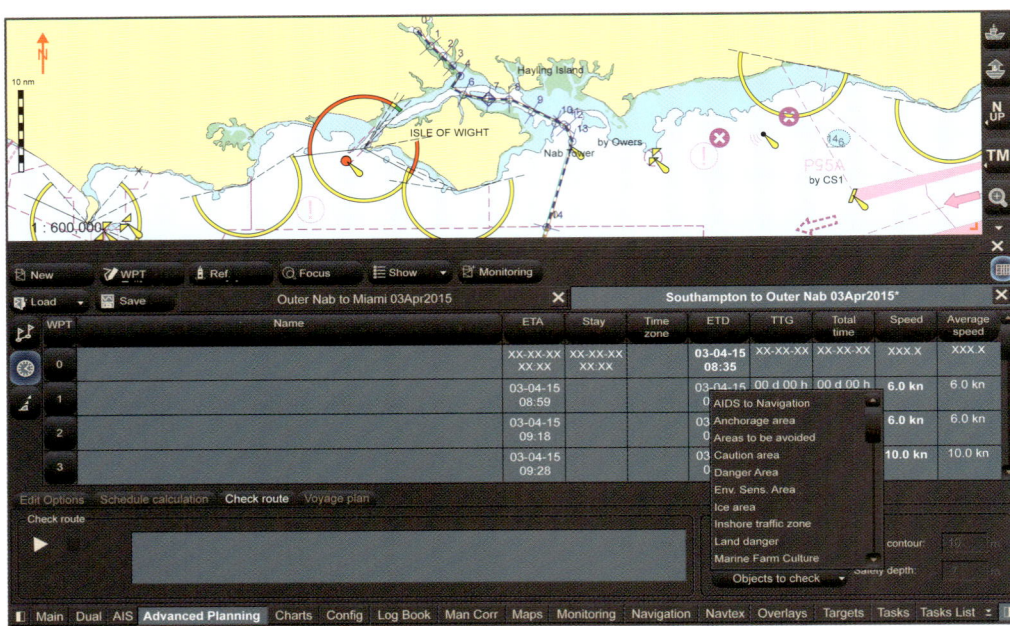

Figure 78: Configuring what areas the route check detects is critical to safe route checking (Transas)

The chart display must also be configured so that potential dangers detected by the check are shown (see EP 2.1.13 Automatic Route Check). Selection of the All Other display category will alleviate this issue. Another factor that must be considered is the ability, on some ECDIS, to select between conducting the route check on all chart scales or the best scale charts only. Although a route check conducted on only the best scale charts will undoubtedly be quicker and highlight fewer errors, it will not detect inconsistencies between different chart scales of the same area. Consequently, dangers and errors can easily be missed (see Figures 79 and 80). It is therefore recommended that the route check incorporates all ENC scales.

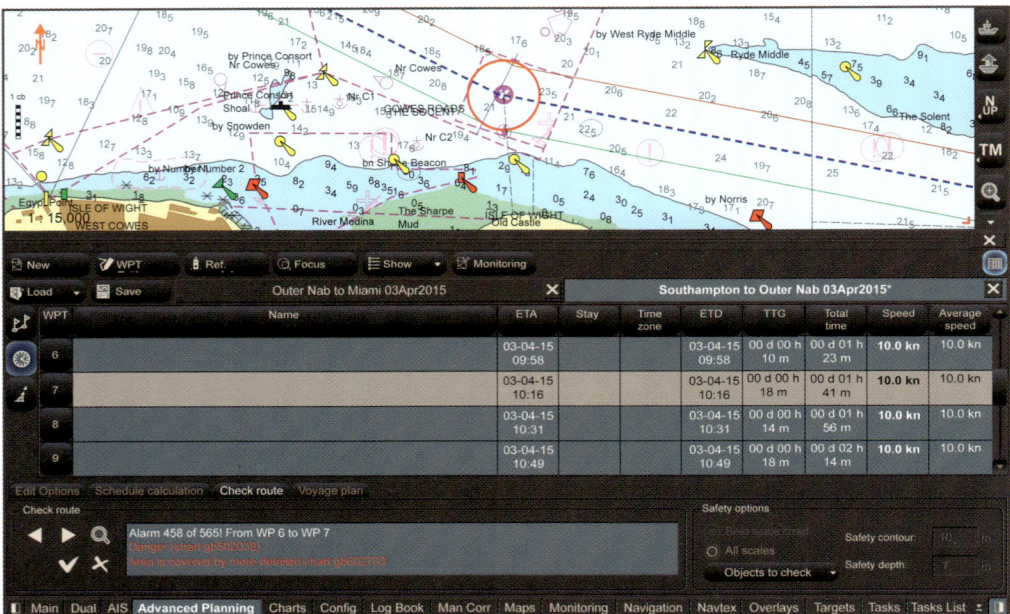

Figure 79: Checking a route on all chart scales can highlight discrepancies. Here, an isolated danger that is a danger to own ship has been located on a scale 5 chart (red circle) (Transas)

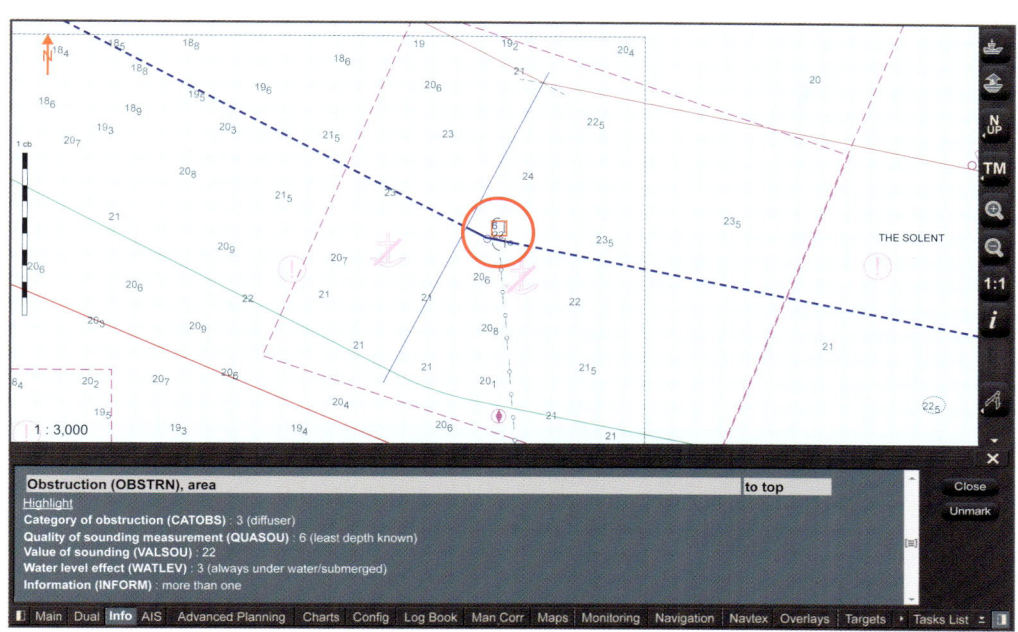

Figure 80: On inspection of the scale 6 chart, the object is no longer displayed as an isolated danger that is a danger to own ship, but an isolated danger deemed not dangerous to navigation. This is most likely a programming error, but it illustrates the need to conduct a route check on all chart scales (Transas)

> Supplementary information can be loaded for the route check, although it should be noted that any mariner's navigational objects containing the danger attribute will be highlighted during the check, where it meets the XTD. This has the advantage of reassuring the NO that they will be detected, but also can make checking the route more onerous.

3.5.2 Conducting the Route Check

Load the planned route and activate the route check function on all chart scales. ECDIS will now check, within the stipulated XTD of the entire route, for potential dangers on all installed ENCs that cover the geographical area. This may take a while if the route is long, as a large quantity of charts will need to be checked. When the check is complete, all potential dangers will be available for viewing. Some systems may list this information according to the relevant leg affected. It should be possible to view an individual danger, which in turn will be highlighted by the system so it can be differentiated from other dangers (see Figure 81). When doing so, it may be necessary to perform a cursor pick on highlighted dangers to ascertain further information (see Figures 82-86). Some detected dangers can be disregarded, while others will require revision of the route, normally facilitated within the route check function itself. When editing is complete, the modification will need to be checked. Some systems may provide the ability to check individual legs for this purpose, although it may be necessary to conduct a check of the entire route again where this function does not exist. The automatic check is complete when all dangers have been analysed and either disregarded or the route amended and rechecked.

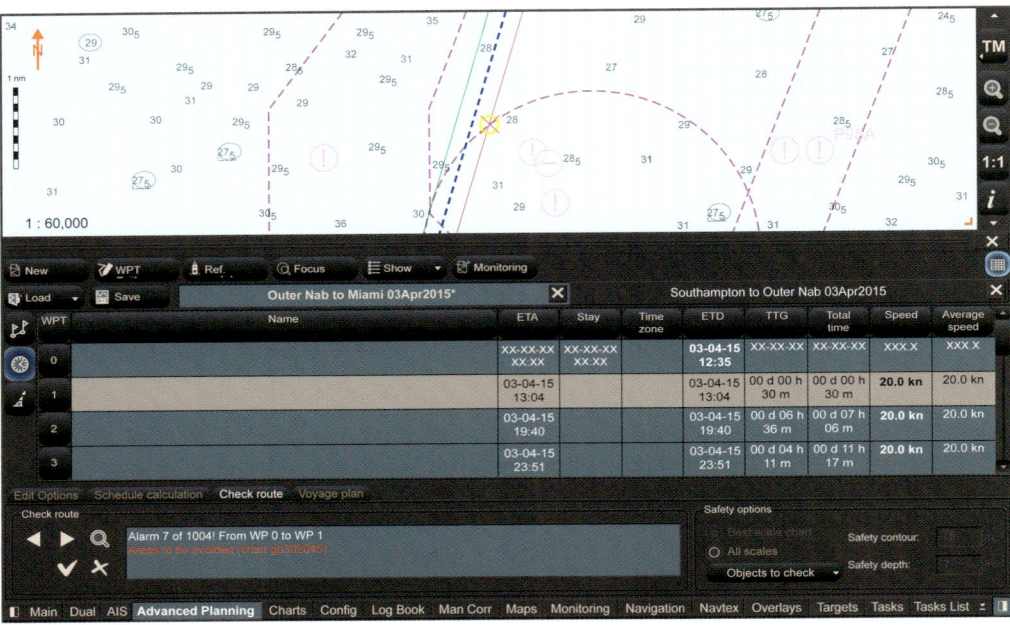

Figure 81: The extent of detected areas and associated information may not be automatically displayed, in which case it will be necessary to use the cursor pick function... (Transas)

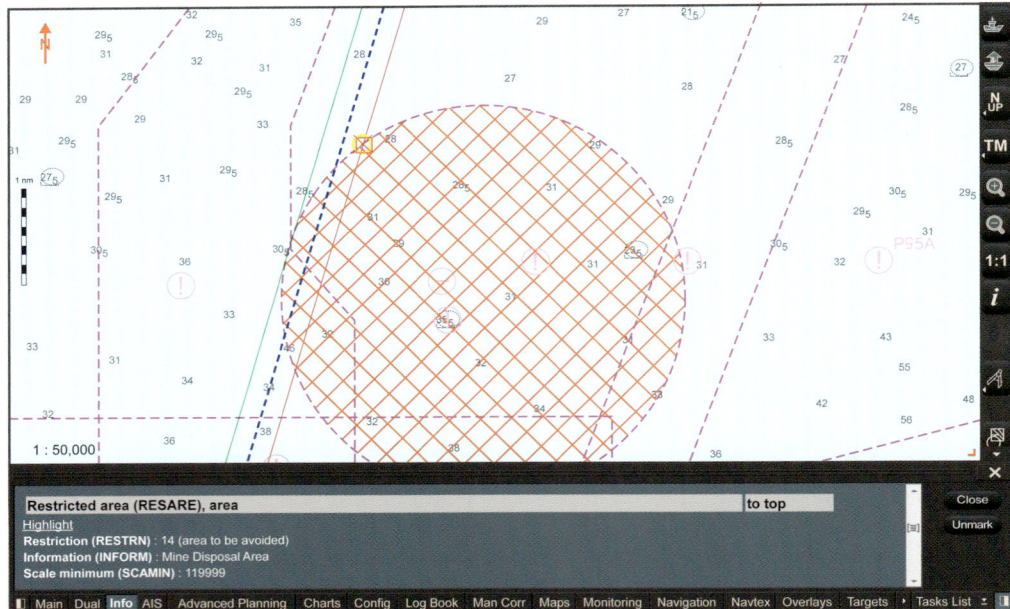

Figure 82: ...the extent of the detected area is now displayed (Transas)

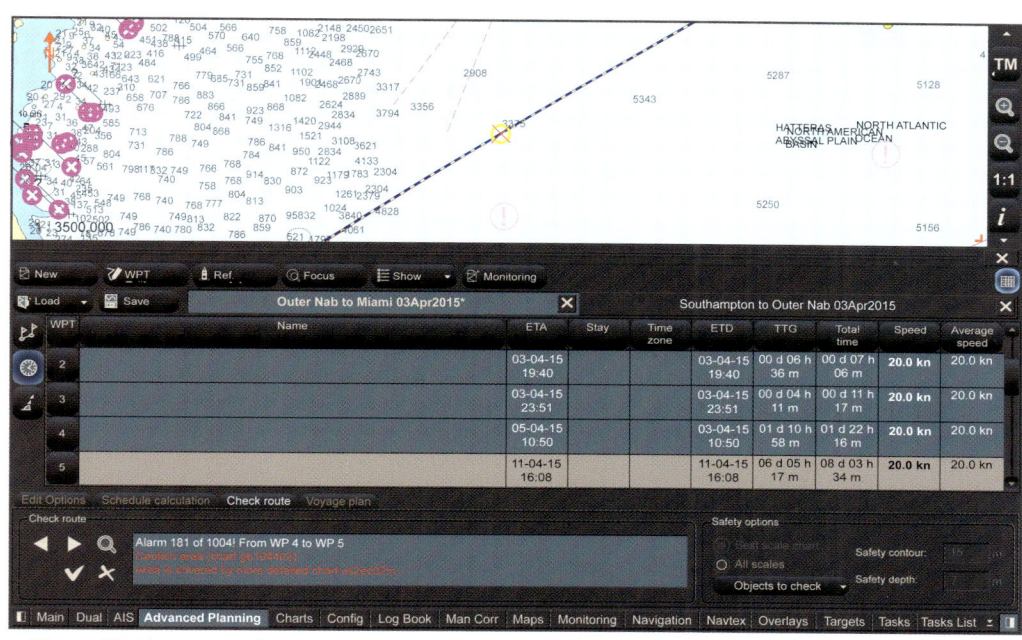

Figure 83: Here, a caution area has been detected, but no further information about the detected danger is available graphically (Transas)

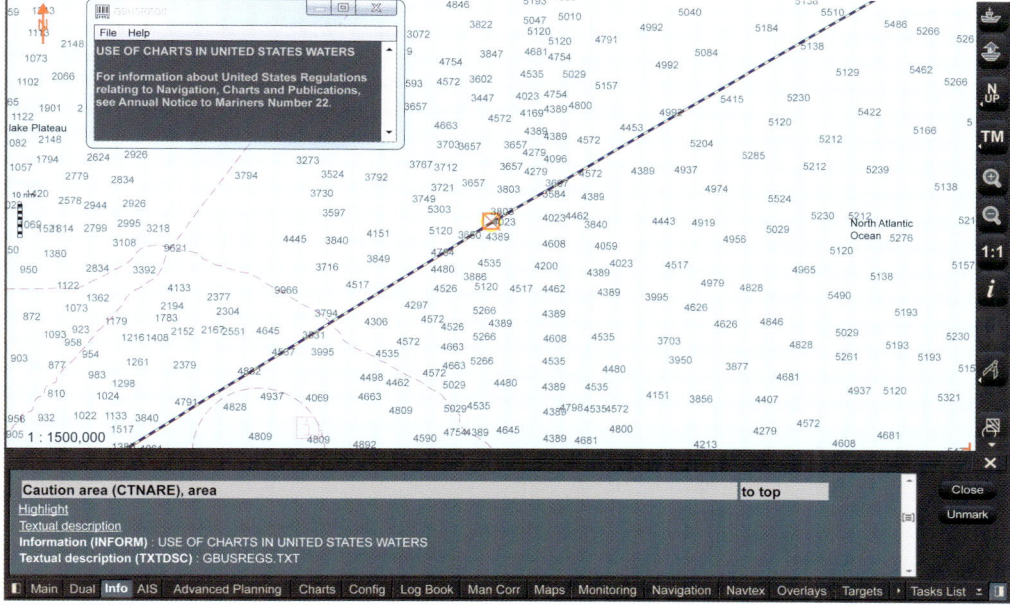

Figure 84: The cursor pick function provides the reason. Hopefully this requirement would have been identified during the appraisal (Transas)

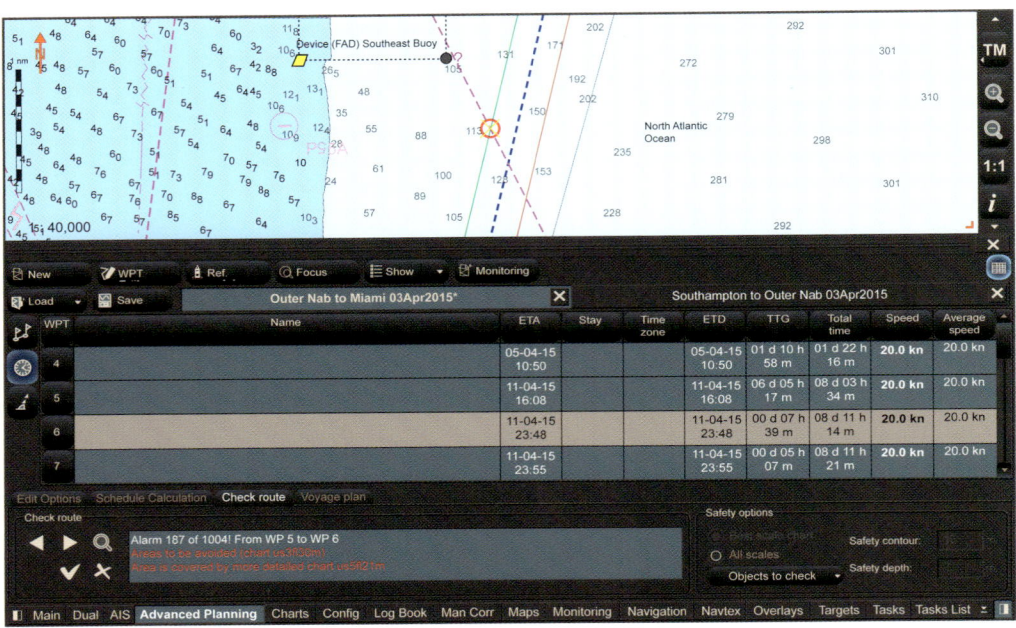

Figure 85: Here, the border of a restricted area has been highlighted... (Transas)

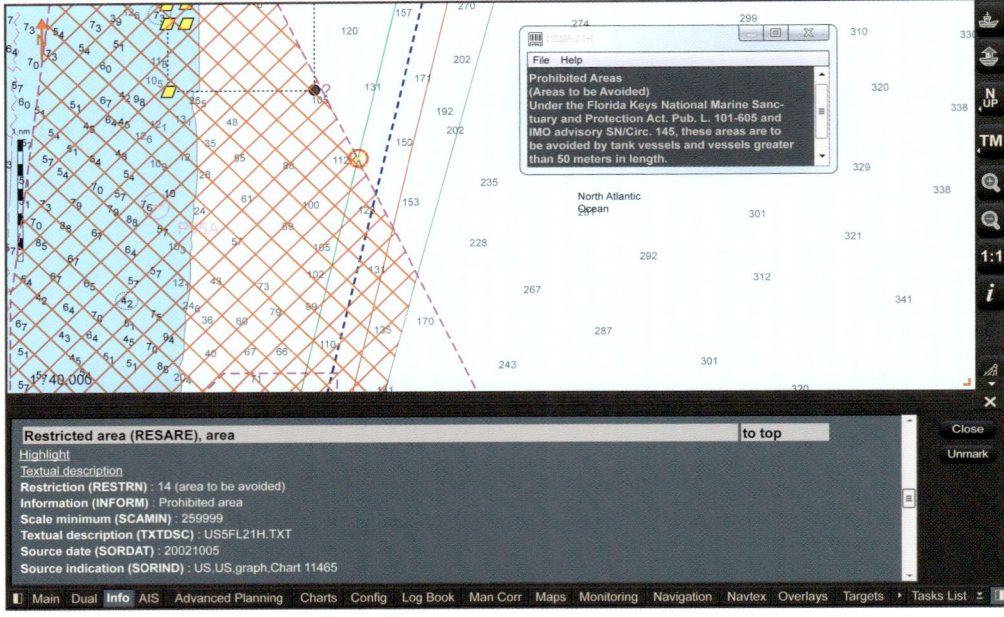

Figure 86: ...the reason for the restriction is available via cursor pick. The route may need to be edited around this area (Transas)

The nature and quantity of parameters that the automatic route check seeks to detect means that even the shortest of routes may result in large quantities of detected dangers. If the route check does not list any detected dangers, then this may be an indication that settings have not been correctly configured. The most likely cause is that no value has been set for XTD, but it may also be that the check has failed to scrutinise all chart scales available. If this occurs, set the XTD to an appropriate value and, where available, set the scale of charts to be checked to cover 'all scales' and run the check again. A route check should be performed prior to executing a route and on the following occasions:

- Following modification of a route

- following a chart update

- following a change in the safety contour value.

There are many frustrating aspects associated with the automatic route check. For example, when an area considered a danger is detected, many ECDIS will only highlight the affected section of the XTD and not the full extent of the area. This means additional investigation is required to establish the boundaries of an area around which the route must be modified, which can be time consuming.

3.5.3   Visual Check

The automatic route check is a useful tool in the planning process, but it is not an infallible safety check. Documented anomalies reported in some ECDIS, where dangers have not been detected during the check, is a reason why it should not be relied upon. Although the majority of known anomalies have been cured, undetected anomalies may still exist. Therefore, careful visual inspection of the entire planned route should also be conducted. This should be undertaken using appropriate scale charts and the All Other display category to confirm that the route, and any deviations from it, is clear of dangers. The presence of any anomalies should be reported immediately to the relevant authority. Once the visual check has been completed, save any changes to the route.

The automatic route check will not detect charted dangers on an RNC. If gaps in ENC coverage are being filled with RNCs, then these will have to be checked visually.

The detailed passage plan can now be presented to the Master for consideration and approval, prior to the commencement of the passage. The Master's scrutiny of the detailed plan is an essential additional safety check and modifications may be required as a result. Good use of ECDIS or a planning terminal should be made to brief the Master, where any critical phase of the passage can be better explained. Key points that may be appropriate in the Master's brief are as follows:

3.6 Detailed Briefing

- Overall speed, time (ETD, ETA) and distance

    - any elements that have changed significantly from the feasibility brief

    - changes to speed en-route

    - estimated fuel consumption

- route and any alternatives

    - areas where it is planned to cross the safety contour

    - locations where concentrations of fishing vessels are likely to be encountered

    - main shipping routes impinging on planned route

    - marine environment protection measures

- MARPOL
- no go lines
- other
  - anti-piracy
  - change of time zones and locations
  - known meteorological data
  - predicted currents with their likely strength and direction
  - sunrise and sunset times and locations
  - territorial sea boundaries.

On completion of the brief, the approval of the plan by the Master should be recorded and all workings retained for Port State Inspections and ISM, in a workbook or electronically. Route tables can be printed for this purpose. Lock or protect the route with a password if necessary, and save a backup in case it is erased in error.

Although some changes to the plan are inevitable, never underestimate the value of sound planning. The more complete the preparation, the easier the execution. Remember that ECDIS is far from infallible, so never solely rely on it. Instead, go to great lengths to prove that the information it provides, particularly charted and positional information, is accurate.

References

Organisation	Source
IHO	S-52 Annex A, IHO Presentation Library for ECDIS Edition 4.0.0
	S-52 Specifications for Chart Content and Display Aspects of ECDIS
	S-52 Appendix 1, Guidance on Updating the Electronic Navigational Chart
	S-52 Appendix 2, Colours and Symbols Specifications for ECDIS
	S-57 Maintenance Document No. 8
	S-57 Transfer Standard for Digital Hydrographic Data
	S-63 IHO Data Protection Scheme
IMO	Resolution MSC.232(82) Revised Performance Standards for ECDIS
	Circular 207, Differences Between RCDS and ECDIS
	Circular 255, Additional Guidance on Chart Datums and the Accuracy of Positions on Charts
	Circular 266/Rev.1, Maintenance of ECDIS Software
	Circular 312, Operating Anomalies Identified Within ECDIS
	Circular 1391, Operating Anomalies Identified Within ECDIS
NOAA	US Chart 1

SECTION **3**
Annexes

Annexes

Annex A – Passage Planning Checklists

Checklist A: Questions		References/Remarks
General Information		
1. Is the name of the port(s) known correctly and been confirmed by the Master?	☑ ☐	→ ....
2. Will the ship be loaded or in ballast? (For ships manoeuvring data)	☐	→ Loaded/In Ballast
3. Has the Chief Engineer advised of bunkering requirements?	☐	→ ....
4. Has the Chief Officer advised of draught and stability?	☐	→ ....
5. Are there any port/pilot/agent/charterer's instructions for the intended passage?	☐	→ ....
6. Does the company have any special instructions pertaining to the route?	☐	→ ....
7. Has the Master given any particular instructions?	☐	→ ....
8. Is the vessel required to use weather routeing? Name of service.	☐	→ ....
9. Are there any MARPOL requirements to be allowed for?	☐	→ ....
10. Are there any ballast water exchange requirements to be allowed for?	☐	→ ....
11. Are there any advisories from the Flag State or task forces?	☐	→ ....
12. Have different route options been prepared and presented to the Master?	☐	→ ....
13. Has the Master finalised the route choice? Chosen option?	☐	→ ....
14. Has the ship been to the present destination port(s) in the past? (If so, the record of previous passage can help identify the route and the navigation officer can construct a new route with amendments)	☐	→ Date of Voyage/Copy of previous Passage Plan → ....
15. Is there any Watchkeeping officer on board who has already been to that area/port?	☐	→ Name/Record of Information obtained → ....

Checklist B: Questions		References/Remarks
a) Vessel		
1. Is there any bunker port diversion to consider bunkering?	☐	→ Yes/No (If YES, Sheet No.) ....
2. Has the pilot card been updated? (If possible, obtain a copy and attach with passage plan)	☐	→ Yes/No (If YES, Sheet No.) ....
3. Would the ship have sufficient UKC?	☐	→ UKC .... m/ft
4. Has the pilot boarding area been considered for manoeuvring to provide lee for pilot boat?	☐	→ Yes/No (If YES, Sheet No.) ....
5. Are there any overhead cables/bridges in the passage for consideration of air-draught?	☐	→ Yes/No (If YES, Sheet No.) ....
6. Are there any special cargo condition/requirements that may affect the passage plan?	☐	→ Yes/No (If YES, Sheet No.) ....
b) Weather		
1. Does the plan take meteorological conditions into account?	☐	→ ....
2. Have the latest weather forecasts/warnings been obtained, checked and allowed for?	☐	→ .... **Sheet No.** ....
3. Does the ship follow advice from any weather routeing service?	☐	→ .... **Sheet No.** ....
4. Have the latest navigational warnings been taken into account?	☐	→ ....
c) Watchkeeping and Other Personnel		
1. Has the requirement for OOW/lookout doubling up watches been considered with respect to adverse weather/restricted visibility/critical approaches?	☐	→ .... **Sheet No.** ....
2. Have the crew calling points for anchor/berthing stations, piracy watches been established and noted on chart/passage plan?	☐	→ .... **Sheet No.** ....
3. Have the rest hours for watchkeepers been considered?	☐	→ .... **Sheet No.** ....
d) Passage		
1. Are there any mandatory ship reporting schemes?	☐	→ ....
2. Has the position of pilot boarding/disembarkation points been established?	☐	→ ....
3. Has clock adjustment with respect to local times been considered and times/positions noted on chart to advance/retard clocks?	☐	→ ....
4. Has condition and availability of anchorage berths been considered?	☐	→ ....
5. Is risk assessment carried out for predicted areas of danger?	☐	→ ....

Checklist C: Questions		References/Remarks
Publications		
1. Is there any requirement for the use of local publications/navigational charts?	☐	→ Yes/No (If YES, Sheet No.) ....
2. Are there any local publications required and available for departure and destination port? How to obtain the same?	☐	→ Yes/No (If YES, Sheet No.) ....
3. Are the following publications present on board and corrected up to date?		
a. Chart Catalogue (NP 131)	☐	→ Edn. ... ...
b. Navigational Charts - including largest scale available	☐	→ Corrected to ANM ... ...
c. Routeing Charts	☐	→ Edn. ... ...
d. Admiralty Notices to Mariners/Annual Summary	☐	→ Latest ANM on board ... ...
e. Sailing Directions	☐	→ Edn. ... ... Corrected to ANM ....
f. Tide Tables	☐	→ Edn. ... ...
g. Tidal Stream Atlases	☐	→ Edn. ... ...
h. List of Lights and Fog Signals	☐	→ Edn. ... ... Corrected to ANM ....
i. List of Radio Signals	☐	→ Edn. ... ... Corrected to ANM ....
j. Guide to Port Entry	☐	→ Edn. ... ...
k. The Mariner's Handbook	☐	→ Edn. ... ... Corrected to ANM ....
l. Ocean Passages for the World	☐	→ Edn. ... ... Corrected to ANM ....
m. Ships Routeing Guide (IMO)	☐	→ Edn. ... ...
n. Load line chart	☐	→ Edn. ... ...
o. Other	☐	→ Edn. ... ...
4. Additional Publications		
a. MSNs, MGNs, MINs	☐	→ Location on bridge ....
b. Manuals for all the navigational equipment on bridge	☐	→ Location on bridge ....
c. International Code of Signals	☐	→ Edn. ... ...
d. Admiralty/other Distance Tables	☐	→ Edn. ... ...
e. Chart Correction Log (NP133A)	☐	→ Edn. ... ...
f. IALA System of Buoyage (NP735)	☐	→ Edn. ... ...
g. Symbols and Abbreviations (BA Chart 5011)	☐	→ Edn. ... ...
h. Additional	☐	→ ....

103

Annexes

Section 3

Checklist D: Questions		References/Remarks
Plan		
1. Have the following been marked/drawn on the chart:		
a) Margins of safety as required by the Master/Company.	☐	→ ....
b) Predicated areas of danger and no-go areas.	☐	→ marked on charts
c) Minimum under keel clearance required for each leg of the passage, particularly in shallow waters.	☐	→ marked on charts → References...............
d) Courses as recommended by local/international regulations, company and the Master's instructions.	☐	→ References ....
e) Waypoints and wheel over points.	☐	→ marked on charts
f) Waypoint number on each waypoint, with wheel over info	☐	→ marked on charts
g) Radar conspicuous objects, eg cliffs, hills, RACONs, etc.	☐	→ marked on charts
h) Transits, clearing bearings, clearing marks	☐	→ marked on charts
i) Points for and cross index range (CIR) for parallel indexing (PI).	☐	→ .... **Sheet No.** ....
j) Position on chart where additional navigation aids are required to be switched on	☐	→ marked on charts
k) Abort points and points of no-return	☐	→ .... **Sheet No.** ....
l) Tidal streams and currents.	☐	→ .... **Sheet No.** ....
m) Sequence of charts for the passage.	☐	→ marked on charts
n) Position from where to move onto next chart along with chart number	☐	→ marked on charts
o) VTS or other reporting points marked on the chart and noted in the passage plan sheet.	☐	→ .... **Sheet No.** ....
p) Pilot boarding position and alternate pilot boarding position in case of adverse weather.	☐	→ References............... ....
q) Speed reduction points.	☐	→ .... **Sheet No.** ....
r) Notices to engine room.	☐	→ .... **Sheet No.** ....
s) Point where call is given to ship's crew for anchor/berthing stations.	☐	→ .... **Sheet No.** ....
t) Specific meteorological information related to any area, eg haze, dust storms, areas of restricted visibility	☐	→ marked on charts → References.....................
u) Navigational warnings, temporary and Preliminary corrections from notices to mariners.	☐	→ marked on charts → References.....................
v) Areas of special marine environmental protection consideration.	☐	→ marked on charts → References.....................
2. Have the primary and secondary means of position fixing been agreed upon?	☐	→ Recorded in passage plan sheet
3. Have the position plotting intervals been agreed upon for each leg?	☐	→ Recorded in passage plan sheet
4. Has datum on navigational chart been identified along with corrections stated to apply for WGS84?	☐	→ Recorded in passage plan sheet

Checklist E: Questions		References/Remarks
Contingency Plans 1. Are there any contingency plans available for the following?		
• Failure of electronic navigational aids	☐	→ .... Sheet No. ....
• Man overboard	☐	→ .... Sheet No. ....
• Fire	☐	→ .... Sheet No. ....
• Steering gear failure	☐	→ .... Sheet No. ....
• Main engine failure	☐	→ .... Sheet No. ....
• Helicopter operations	☐	→ .... Sheet No. ....
• Radar/ARPA failures	☐	→ .... Sheet No. ....
• Piracy/armed robbery/terrorist activity	☐	→ .... Sheet No. ....
• Distress	☐	→ .... Sheet No. ....
• Unavailability of pilot/OOW/lookout/helmsman	☐	→ .... Sheet No. ....
• Adverse weather/visibility/ice/TRS	☐	→ .... Sheet No. ....
2. Are all officers and crew fully familiar with relevant bridge equipment and procedures	☐	→ Yes / No, If not reference to company procedure ....
3. Have OOWs and crew been briefed about the passage plan.	☐	→ Signature on passage plan sheet
4. Have all OOWs seen, understood and signed the passage plan?	☐	→ Signature on passage plan sheet
5. Has the Master reviewed and approved the plan?	☐	→ Signature on passage plan sheet

Checklist F: Questions		References/Remarks
Briefings and Approval		
1. Are all officers and crew fully familiar with relevant bridge equipment and procedures	☐	→ Yes / No, If not reference to company procedure ....
2. Have OOWs and crew been briefed about the passage plan.	☐	→ Signature on passage plan sheet
3. Have all OOWs seen, understood and signed the passage plan?	☐	→ Signature on passage plan sheet
4. Has the Master reviewed and approved the plan?	☐	→ Signature on passage plan sheet

Annex B – ECDIS Planning Checklist

System Configuration

Chart Installation

[ ] Official chart formats

  – SOLAS compliant

  – ENCs of an appropriate scale and accuracy

[ ] RCDS mode

  – appropriate RNCs

  – appropriate folio of paper charts

  – risk assessment

[ ] Contingency chart provision

[ ] Time to procure and receive

[ ] Time to install

Updates

Safety notices

[ ] Notices to mariners (NM)

[ ] Temporary and preliminary notices (T&P NM, AIO)

[ ] Local NM

[ ] Radio navigational warnings (NAVAREAS & WZs)

[ ] Time to update all ECDIS

Chart permits and licence

[ ] Relevant ENC and RNC permits held on board

[ ] Chart permits up to date

[ ] Chart permit expiry

[ ] ECDIS licence expiry

ECDIS

[ ] Latest software

[ ] Generic and type specific training

Software Configuration

ECDIS software

[ ]   Latest manufacturer's software patch is installed

[ ]   Latest presentation library (IHO S-52)

[ ]   Latest data protection standards (IHO S-63)

[ ]   Read the latest IMO guidance on ECDIS anomalies

[ ]   Report ECDIS anomalies to the appropriate authority

Display Configuration

Display mode

[ ]   Display set-up

    –   unload all routes

    –   unload all manual constructs

    –   full screen (hide sidebar)

    –   day white palette

[ ]   Chart settings

    –   Display mode 'all other'

    –   chart priority ENC

    –   chart autoload ON

    –   chart autoscale ON

    –   scale minimum ON

    –   AIO layer ON

    –   shallow pattern ON

    –   full light lines ON

    –   show correction ON

    –   chart boundaries ON

    –   show isolated dangers in shallow water ON

    –   traditional chart symbols or simplified

    –   traditional areas or symbolised

    –   two or four colour shades

[ ]   Safety settings

    –   Safety depth (see below for guidance)

    –   safety contour (see below for guidance)

- shallow contour
- deep contour

[ ] Route settings
- Display of cross track limit (XTL)
- display of distances
- display of true courses
- display of waypoint names
- display of turn radius

Safety values

[ ] Safety depth

[ ] safety contour

[ ] safety height

Other values

[ ] Shallow contour

[ ] deep contour

Route Planning

New route

[ ] Berth to berth

[ ] Areas where the services of a pilot will be used

[ ] Name the route

[ ] Locate start and end points

Adding waypoints

[ ] Add waypoint at start location

[ ] Construct route on small scale

[ ] Define leg properties as rhumb line or Great Circle

[ ] If Great Circle divide leg into rhumb lines

Adjusting Waypoints

Regarding the vessel

[ ] Draught, available depth of water and minimum UKC

[ ] Manoeuvring characteristics

[ ] Effect of course alteration on draught and turning circle

- Planned speed
- effect of expected tidal stream
- effect of expected current
- increase in draught due to squat and heel effect

[ ] Positions where change in machinery status is required

[ ] Positions where additional manning is required

Regarding the route

[ ] Safety and efficiency of navigation

[ ] Depth of water

[ ] Safe speed and proximity of navigational hazards

[ ] Use of ships' routeing, reporting systems and VTS

[ ] Protection of the marine environment

[ ] Avoidance of danger areas

[ ] Alterations of speed en-route

[ ] Location of course alterations

[ ] Limitations of night passage

[ ] Tidal restrictions

[ ] Adequate cross track limit (XTL)

[ ] Contingency planning

- Deep water
- port of refuge or safe anchorage in emergency
- shore-based emergency response arrangements
- nature of the cargo and of the emergency itself

[ ] Method and frequency of position fixing

- Primary and secondary fixing options
- areas where accuracy of position fixing is critical
- areas of maximum reliability of position fixing
- availability of relative navigation technique visual and radar fixing
  - Radar image overlay

    ○   parallel indices

    ○   astronomical observations

[ ]   Save route

Quality control checks

[ ]   Visual check of ENC

    –   Isolated dangers outside of safety contour

    –   gaps in ENC coverage

    –   CATZOCs and accuracy of ENC

    –   comparison of equivalent RNC where possible

[ ]   Cursor pick

    –   Interrogate symbols

    –   interrogate objects and areas for more information

[ ]   AIO layer

    –   T&P NM information

Route table

[ ]   Latitude and longitude of waypoint

[ ]   XTL (port and starboard)

[ ]   Arrival radius (for use with track control systems)

[ ]   Planned speed

[ ]   Leg property (RL or GC)

[ ]   Rate of turn

[ ]   Turn radius

[ ]   Time zone

[ ]   Course

[ ]   Distance

[ ]   ETD

[ ]   ETA

[ ]   Name waypoints where necessary

[ ]   Draught (provided on some systems)

[ ]   UKC (provided on some systems)

Route Check

Automatic check

Occasions for check

[　]　After route planning

[　]　After modification of a route

[　]　After a chart update

Configuration

[　]　All other display mode

Detected dangers

[　]　Route crosses own ship's safety contour

[　]　Point objects

　　　　– 　Fixed or floating aid to navigation

　　　　– 　isolated danger

[　]　Boundaries of a prohibited or geographic area

　　　　– 　Traffic separation zone

　　　　– 　inshore traffic zone

　　　　– 　restricted area

　　　　– 　caution area

　　　　– 　offshore production area

　　　　– 　areas to be avoided

　　　　– 　user defined areas to be avoided

　　　　– 　anchorage area

Actions following check

[　]　View listed dangers

[　]　Use cursor pick to view additional information

[　]　Modify route to avoid listed dangers

[　]　Disregard dangers deemed not relevant

[　]　Re-check relevant legs following modifications

[　]　If gaps in ENC coverage visually check RNCs

[　]　Visual check of entire route on appropriate scale charts

[　]　Save route

Supplementary Information

Manual constructs

Highlight

[ ] Planned changes of safety depth and safety contour

[ ] No go lines

[ ] International regulations, codes and guidelines

[ ] Ships' routeing, reporting systems and VTS

[ ] Planned time zone changes

[ ] Tidal diamonds

[ ] True direction of the planned route

[ ] All areas of danger

[ ] Areas of limited data

[ ] Areas of special interest and concern

[ ] Areas of marine environmental protection

[ ] Points of 'no return' and contingencies

[ ] Changes in IALA systems of maritime buoyage

[ ] Areas where accuracy of position fixing is critical

[ ] Areas of maximum reliability of position fixing

[ ] Weather concerns and measures to be taken

Detailed Briefing

[ ] Overall speed, time (ETD, ETA) and distance

– Significant changes from the feasibility brief

– changes to speed en-route

– passage graph

[ ] Route and alternatives

– No go lines

– likely concentrations of fishing vessels

– main shipping routes impinging on planned route

– marine environment protection measures

– MARPOL

[ ] Other

    –   Sunrise and sunset times and locations

    –   change of time zones and locations

    –   predicted currents, likely strength and direction

    –   known meteorological data

    –   territorial sea boundaries

    –   anti-piracy areas

Annex C – Parallel Indexing

Parallel indexing is an effective way of monitoring a vessel's progress along a preselected track using a radar.

As a vessel moves on its chosen heading, fixed objects in its radar vicinity appear to be moving in a reciprocal direction to this motion. This technique provides the radar observer with a real time view of the ship's lateral position relative to the planned track. The approach can be used in all conditions of visibility to monitor the vessel's cross-track movement.

The following must be confirmed before employing the radar in this way:

1. The performance of the radar must be checked at regular intervals.

2. Gyro error must be checked.

3. Heading marker should be in alignment with the ship's fore and aft line.

4. The accuracy of range rings and the variable range marker (VRM) should be checked against a good fix.

5. The fixed target that is to be tracked must be correctly identified.

Parallel indexing provides an active method of assessing the vessel's progress continuously and immediately without the need for visual bearings that provide historic data due to the associated delay of assessment.

Parallel indexing is particularly useful in reduced visibility, areas of high traffic density, coastal and pilotage stages of a voyage.

The vessel is shown to be maintaining the required track, with the target (point of land) moving from position 1 to position 3, down the starboard side of the vessel following the PI line. The ship is following a ground track of 270°T.

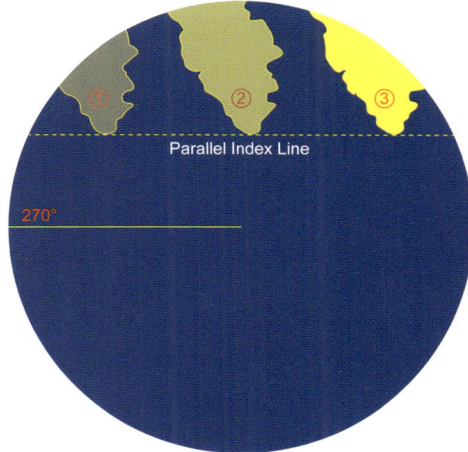

The ship is shown to be setting towards the shore. The point of land is moving inside the PI line and getting progressively closer to the ship. The ship is following a ground track of 280°T.

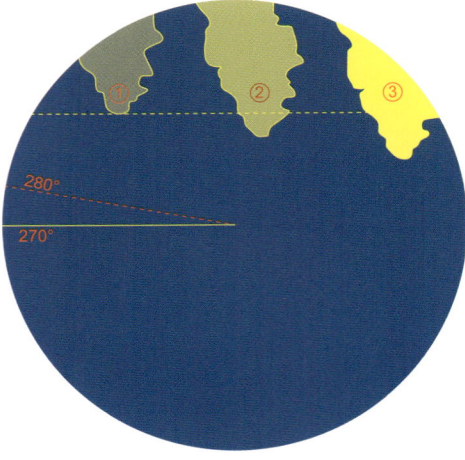

The ship is shown to be setting away from the shore. The point of land is moving outside the PI line and getting progressively further from the ship. The ship is following a ground track of 262°T.

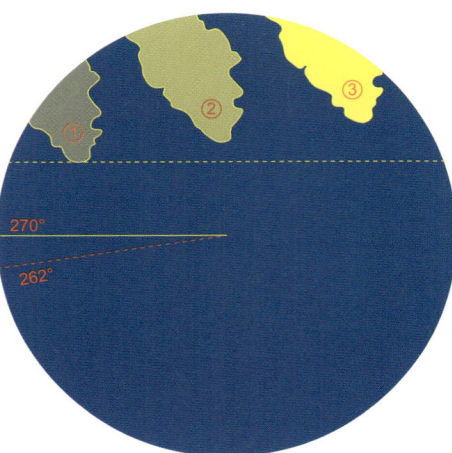

Cross Index Range (CIR)

This is based on the lateral distance of the planned track from a selected object. It can be used with parallel indexing to provide a safe 'channel' when the ship needs to move from the charted course line. The following method can be used:

- Identify the hazards and mark the limiting danger lines and tracks.

- select a suitable charted object

- draw a line on the chart parallel to the planned track on the inner edge of the selected object

- mark maximum margins of safety (MOS) on either side, or on the side with off-lying dangers

- measure the perpendicular distance from track to this line. This distance is the CIR

- then measure distances for the MOS.

The MOS port distance is treated as a 'not less than' (NLT) distance from the danger and MOS starboard as a 'not more than' (NMT) distance from the index line. Mark these three lines on the radar screen as index and MOS lines, either electronically or on the plotter using VRM and cursor

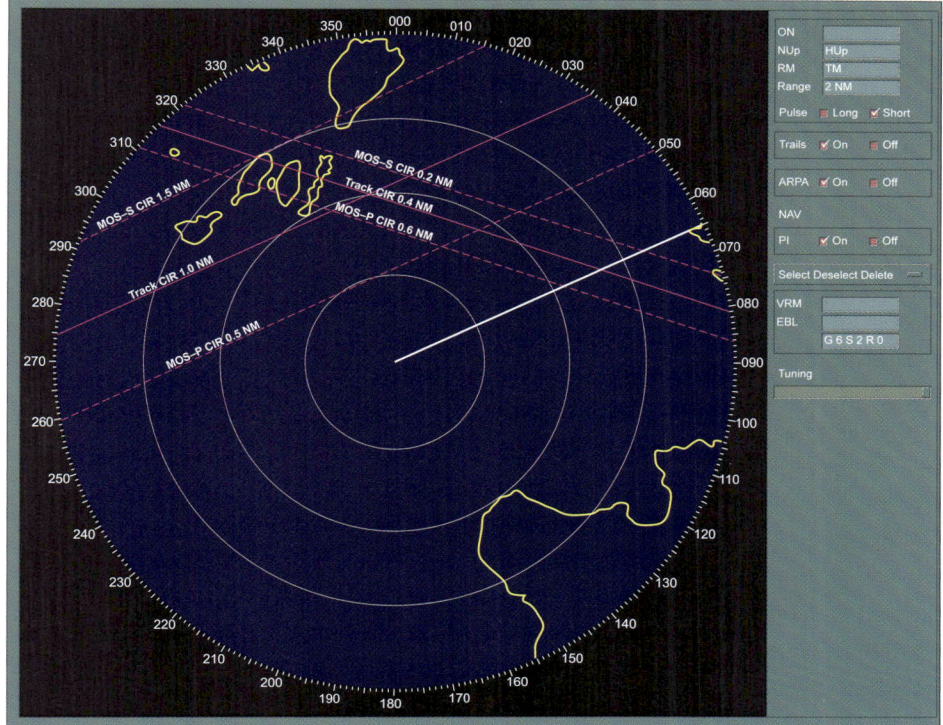

Radar Display with Track, CIR and MOS Index Lines

By using additional PI lines, alterations can be incorporated and include the use of wheel over positions marked on the chart.

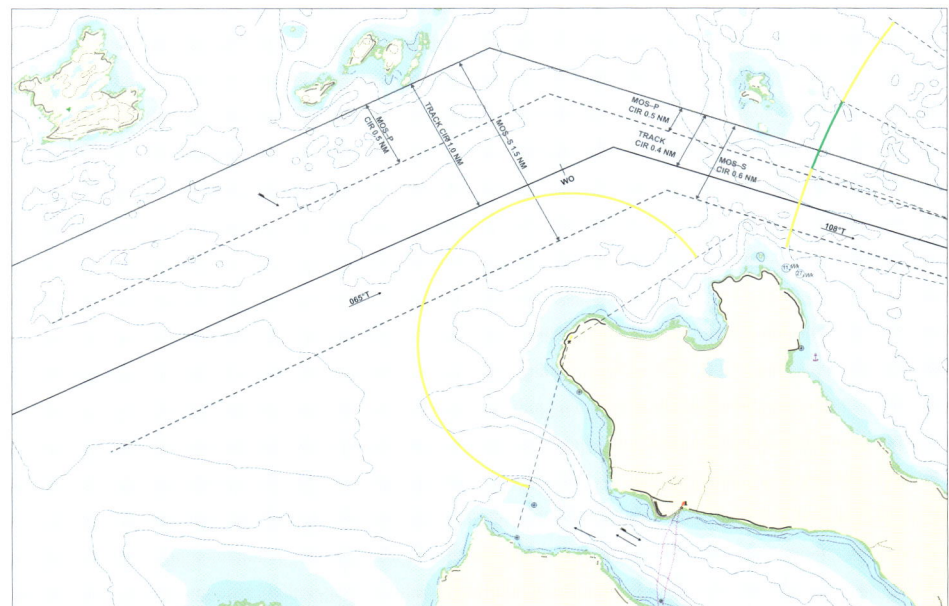

Parallel index lines incorporating the next course line

Integration with ECDIS

Where the radar display is integrated with an ECDIS, the practice of parallel indexing continues to enable the navigator to monitor the ship's position relative to the planned track and additionally provides a means of continuously monitoring the positional integrity of the ECDIS system.

Precautions

It is important to remember that parallel index lines drawn on reflection plotters apply to one range scale only. In addition to all other precautions necessary for the safe use of radar information, particular care must therefore be taken when changing range scales.

The use of parallel indexing does not remove the requirement for position fixing at regular intervals, using all appropriate methods available including visual bearings, since parallel indexing only indicates if the ship is on or off track and not its progress along the track.

Annex D – Passage Plan Work Sheet

PASSAGE PLAN																	
Vessel:	**Prepared by:**																
Voyage No:	(Navigation Officer)																
From:	**Date:**																
To:	**Approved by:**																
Berth:	(Master)																
(Name of Berth/Wharf/Anchorage)	**Date:**																
	OOW2:																
	OOW1:																

References: (Write Vol No and Page Nos for quick reference)
Publication Correction: Date .... **ANM No** ....
Sailing Directions: ....
ALRS: ....
ATT: ....
ALLFS: ....
Ocean Passages: ....
NAVTEX Stations: ....
VHF Channels: ....

Drafts
F: ....m
A: ....m

Chart(s)		Waypoints			Course° T	Speed	Eng Order	Distance and Time to go						Min. Depth/UKC m	Parallel Index		WO		Position Fixing			Current Tidal Stream		Master's instructions Hazards Weather Contingency Remarks
Number	Datum	Name	No	Lat				Next Waypoint			Total				Reference Mark	CIR	Reference Mark	Bearing x Range	Frequency (min)	Primary	Secondary	Set	Rate	
				Long				Distance	Time	Distance	Distance	Time												
																				Vis/Radar/GPS	Vis/Radar/GPS			
																				Vis/Radar/GPS	Vis/Radar/GPS			
																				Vis/Radar/GPS	Vis/Radar/GPS			

Annex E – Example of Passage Planning Notes

Leg 7	Dover Strait (Cap Gris-Nez to Sandettié)
On Leg Distance	18 nm
Primary Fixing	Visual/Radar Cap Gris-Nez Fl 5s 29M Varne Light Float Fl R 5s 15M Racon (T) MPC Fl Y 2.5s Racon (O) Sandettié Fl 5s 15M Racon (T)
BA Chart	BA 323, BA 1610, BA 1892, BA 2449
Frequency	10 mins
Cross Checking	GPS
Parallel Indexing	MPC Racon (O) Sandettié Racon (T)
Position/ Lining Up	Deep water route crosses from starboard to the portside of the channel north of the Sandettié SW buoy
Traffic	This area can be very busy with cross channel ferries, including high speed craft, particularly during the summer months. These vessels will normally be trying to cross the TSS at right angles to the direction of traffic flow. Traffic may also join/leave to the North of the lane, towards Dover and the UK coast, and to the South to/from the French coast. Commercial traffic with very different speeds, fishing vessels and recreational craft following the lane can be encountered. A good lookout needs to be maintained to watch for unusual craft, recreational and fishing vessels operating in the separation zone or crossing the straits. During 2012, there were 169 unorthodox crossings, which include swims or rows of the Channel. Each unorthodox crossing will be attended by an escort boat, which may be using AIS-B.
Reporting	

Monitoring	Ch 16/13 and Dover Coastguard on Ch 11
	NAVTEX: Niton [E], Oostende [T]
	
	Traffic Information Messages
		Additionally in reduced visibility
		
		French Broadcasts French Broadcasts
		  hr + 10mins (Ch 13/79) hr + 25mins (Ch 13/79)
		UK Broadcasts UK Broadcasts
		  hr + 40mins (Ch 11) hr + 55mins (Ch 11)

Bridge Manning & Engine Availability	As per ship's passage plan
Tides & Currents	Strong North East/South West
Contingencies	Anchorage space available to the south of the NE-bound lane. Ordinarily, vessels over 50 m in length are prohibited from anchoring in the Calais approche area
Notes	

Annex F – List of Useful Publications

Advanced Navigation Mates/Masters (Witherby Seamanship)

Annual Summary of Notices to Mariners

Anti-Piracy Planning Chart

Bridge Procedures Guide (Marisec, 4th Edition, 2007)

Distance Tables

ECDIS Procedures Guide (Witherby Seamanship 2012)

Guide to ENC Symbols used in ECDIS

Guide to the Practical Use of ENCs

IALA Buoyage System

IMO Resolution A.893(21) Guidelines for Voyage Planning

List of Light and Fog Signals

List of Radio Signals

Mariner's Handbook (UKHO NP100)

Maritime Security Charts

Nautical Almanac

Navigation for Masters (Witherby Seamanship 2012)

Norie's Tables

Ocean Passages for the World (UKHO NP136)

Passage Planning Dover Strait and English Channel (Witherby Seamanship 2013)

Passage Planning Malacca and Singapore Straits (Witherby Seamanship 2013)

Passage Planning Practice (Witherby Seamanship 2006)

Passage Planning Principles (Witherby Seamanship 2012)

Peril at Sea and Salvage (5th Edition, 1998)

Routeing Charts

Routeing Guides

Sailing Directions

Ships Routeing (IMO, 2010)

The ECDIS Manual (Witherby Seamanship 2012)

Tidal Stream Atlases

Tide Tables